Grammar Workbook for

Introductory

Spanish

Third Edition

Domenico Maceri

Allan Hancock College

The McGraw-Hill Companies, Inc.
Primis Custom Publishing

New York St. Louis San Francisco Auckland Bogotá
Caracas Lisbon London Madrid Mexico Milan Montreal
New Delhi Paris San Juan Singapore Sydney Tokyo Toronto

McGraw-Hill Higher Education

A Division of The McGraw-Hill Companies

Grammar Workbook for Introductory Spanish

McGraw-Hill's Primis Custom Publishing consists of products that are produced from camera-ready copy. Peer review, class testing, and accuracy are primarily the responsibility of the author(s).

1 2 3 4 5 6 7 8 9 0 QSR QSR 0 9 8 7 6 5 4 3 2 1 0

ISBN 0-07-244025-2

Sponsoring Editor: Karen Perry
Cover Design: Pat Koch
Printer/Binder: Quebecor World

For Linda

PREFACE

The third edition of *Grammar Workbook for Introductory Spanish* reflects a thorough revision and expansion. Eleven chapters have been added and many others have been restructured. The changes mean that virtually all grammar points introduced in a first-year course are now presented. At the same time, the basic approach has been retained: exercises and easy-to-read explanations of grammar points students encounter in first-year Spanish. Each chapter includes exercises that move from very easy to challenging and review sections which could be used as a means of insuring mastery of the subject. An answer key is provided in the back, so students can check their own progress.

The text can be used as a supplement to any first-year course. After the instructor has given a brief introduction to the grammar point in question, the exercises in this workbook could be assigned as class work or for individual practice outside of class. It could also serve as a review of the material covered in the main textbook, or as individual practice for students who could profit from extra exercises. Although the main audience for the text is first-year students, those at the intermediate level, especially those who pick up the study of Spanish after a lapse of time, will also find it useful in reviewing the grammar points of introductory Spanish.

The explicit study of grammar has lost favor in the last decade or so. Many people feel that students will learn the grammatical concepts inductively by means of "comprehensible input." They are right. Yet, since we have such limited amount of time to provide this input, it becomes essential that we utilize not simply the inductive approach but the deductive one as well. If we have enough supplementary materials for students to work with outside of class—the deductive part— then in class we will be able to concentrate on communication activities.

I am grateful to Ana Calderón, Noé Chávez-Magaña, Bill Cooper, Dolores Doran, Ralph Sutter, and Kendra Tomelloso for their helpful suggestions.

CONTENTS

1 SINGULAR NOUNS AND ARTICLES

- The names for objects, people, animals, and ideas are called **nouns** (*los sustantivos*). All nouns in Spanish can be masculine or feminine.* Generally, nouns ending in **-o** are masculine. Nouns ending in **-a** are feminine.

masculine (*masculino*)	feminine (*femenino*)
libro *book*	casa *house*
taco *taco*	enchilada *enchilada*

- The indefinite article (*el artículo indefinido*) for masculine nouns is **un** (*a, an*). Feminine nouns use **una** (a, an).**

masculine (*masculino*)	feminine (*femenino*)
un libro *a book*	una casa *a house*
un taco *a taco*	una enchilada *an enchilada*

A. Add the appropriate indefinite article **un** or **una**.

1. _____ profesora 2. _____ fiesta 3. _____ libro 4. _____ discoteca 5. _____ secretario 6. _____ laboratorio 7. _____ oficina 8. _____ amigo 9. _____ rancho 10. _____ enchilada

- Nouns ending in **-ción** or **-dad** are feminine.

    una nación (*a nation*); una universidad (*a college, a university*)
- Nouns ending in **-nte** or **-ista** can refer to masculine or feminine. The indefinite article and the context identify if you are talking about a man or a woman.

    un estudiante (*a male student*); una estudiante (*a female student*)

---

* The gender of objects, places, things, and ideas has no relationship with sex. It is simply a grammatical feature. It does not suggest masculine or feminine attributes in the minds of native speakers.

** **Un** and **una** can also translate as **one.** The context makes the distinction.

un dentista (*a male dentist*); una dentista (*a female dentist*)

• Some nouns that refer to people indicate gender (*el género*) by adding an "a" or by changing the final vowel: señor (*gentleman*) señora (*lady*); profesor (*male professor*) profesora (*female professor*); amigo (*male friend*) amiga (*female friend*).

B. Add the appropriate indefinite article **un** or **una**.
1. _____ cliente (*masc.*) 2. _____ condición 3. _____ pianista (*fem.*) 4. _____ socialista (*masc.*) 5. _____ estudiante (*fem.*)
6. _____ sociedad 7. _____ artista (*masc.*) 8. _____ situación
9. _____ ciudad 10. _____ construcción

• Nouns ending in -**e** or consonants can be masculine or feminine. Try to learn the gender as you encounter them. Here are some common ones.

masculine (*masculino*)	feminine (*femenino*)
un hombre *a man*	una noche *a night*
un lápiz *a pencil*	una tarde *an afternoon*
un café *a café*	una clase *a class*
un violín *a violin*	una mujer *a woman*
un doctor *a doctor*	una actriz *an actress*
un saxofón *a saxophone*	una parte *a part*
un actor *an actor*	una madre *a mother*

Exceptions: the following nouns do not follow the rules you have learned:
• **Día, problema, programa, sistema**, and **mapa** end in -**a** but are masculine.
• **Dependienta** and **presidenta** are the feminine forms for **dependiente** and **presidente.**
• The gender (*el género*) of **persona** is feminine, but it may refer to a man or a woman. The context clarifies the meaning.

Singular Nouns and Articles

C. Review. Add the appropriate indefinite article **un** or **una**.

1. _____ secretario 2. _____ noche 3. _____ hombre

4. _____ clase 5. _____ problema 6. _____ oficina

7. _____ papel 8. _____ día 9. _____ café 10. _____ lápiz

11. _____ tarde 12. _____ situación 13. _____ estudiante (*masc.*)

14. _____ pianista (*fem.*) 15. _____ saxofón 16. _____ mujer

• The singular definite articles (*los artículos definidos*) in Spanish are **el** and **la**. Use **el** with masculine nouns and **la** with feminine ones.

masculine	feminine
el libro *the book*	la casa *the house*
el taco *the taco*	la enchilada *the enchilada*

• Definite articles refer to something specific. Indefinite articles indicate something general. Thus, if someone asks you for **a** book, any book will do. If someone asks for a specific book, s/he will ask you for "**the** French book," and only **the** French book will do.

D. Add the appropriate definite articles **el** or **la**.

1. _____ secretaria 2. _____ libro 3. _____ laboratorio

4. _____ amiga 5. _____ rancho 6. _____ oficina

7. _____ papel 8. _____ día 9. _____ café 10. _____ lápiz

11. _____ tarde 12. _____ situación 13. _____ estudiante (*fem.*)

14. _____ pianista (*masc.*) 15. _____ saxofón 16. _____ hombre

E. Review. Translate.

1. a student (*m.*) _____

2. the saxophone _____

3. a pencil _____

4. the house _____

5. a night _____

Singular Nouns and Articles

6. a day _____

7. an office _____

8. the secretary (*m.*) _____

9. the problem _____

10. a woman _____

11. a man _____

12. the afternoon _____

13. the situation _____

14. a city _____

15. a doctor (*m.*) _____

16. the friend (*f.*) _____

17. the artist (*f.*) _____

18. a book _____

19. an elephant _____

20. the dentist (*m.*) _____

2 PLURAL NOUNS AND ARTICLES

	singular (*singular*)	plural (*plural*)
indefinite articles (*artículos indefinidos*)	un *a, an* una *a, an*	unos *some, several, a few* unas *some, several, a few*
definite articles (*artículos definidos*)	el *the* la *the*	los *the* las *the*
nouns (*sustantivos*)	amigo *friend* casa *house*	amigos *friends* casas *houses*

- **Unos** and **unas** can mean "some," "several," or "a few."
- **El, la, los, las** mean "the."
- Add an "**s**" to make the plural of nouns. For nouns ending in a consonant, add **es**: cuaderno-cuadernos; doctor-doctores.
- Nouns ending in -**és** and -**ón** lose the accent mark in the plural: francés-franceses; lección-lecciones.
- The plural masculine form includes a group made entirely of men or men and women. The plural feminine form includes only feminine.
- The plural forms of **lápiz** and **actriz** are **lápices** and **actrices**.*

A. Change from singular to plural.

1. el libro _____

2. la casa _____

3. la persona _____

4. el problema _____

5. el profesor _____

6. una cliente _____

7. una oficina _____

---

* -**ze** in Spanish always becomes -**ce.**

8. un amigo _____

9. una socialista _____

10. un día _____

B. Change from plural to singular.

1. unas amigas _____

2. unos laboratorios _____

3. unos hombres _____

4. unas tardes _____

5. unos dentistas _____

6. las doctoras _____

7. los dependientes _____

8. las partes _____

9. los días _____

10. las situaciones _____

11. los papeles _____

12. los mapas _____

C. Add the appropriate indefinite article (*artículo indefinido*) **unos** or **unas**.

1. _____ secretarios 2. _____ noches 3. _____ hombres

4. _____ clases 5. _____ problemas 6. _____ oficinas

7. _____ papeles 8. _____ días 9. _____ cafés

10. _____ lápices 11. _____ tardes 12. _____ situaciones

13. _____ estudiantes (*masc.*) 14. _____ pianistas (*fem.*)

15. _____ saxofones 16. _____ mujeres

D. Add the appropriate definite article (*artículo definido*) **los** or **las**.

1. _____ secretarias 2. _____ libros 3. _____ laboratorios

4. _____ amigas 5. _____ ranchos 6. _____ oficinas

7. _____ papeles 8. _____ días 9. _____ cafés

10. _____ lápices 11. _____ tardes 12. _____ situaciones

13. _____ estudiantes (*fem.*) 14. _____ pianistas (*masc.*)

15. _____ saxofones 16. _____ hombres

Plural Nouns and Articles

E. Review. Translate.

1. the dentists (*f.*) _____

2. some elephants _____

3. some books _____

4. the artists (*f.*) _____

5. some friends (*f.*) _____

6. a few doctors (*m.*) _____

7. some cities _____

8. the situations _____

9. the afternoons _____

10. some men _____

11. some women _____

12. the problems _____

13. the secretaries (*m.*) _____

14. some offices _____

15. some days _____

16. the nights _____

17. several houses _____

18. some pencils _____

19. the saxophones _____

20. some students (*m.*) _____

TIPS

1. Remember that the article is pronounced quickly with the noun that follows it. Don't pause between article and noun.
2. The noun is more important than the article. The article has some meaning, but it must be used with the noun.

Plural Nouns and Articles

3 SUBJECT PRONOUNS

Study the subject pronouns (*los pronombres personales*) very well and then do the exercises.

Singular	Plural
yo-I	**nosotros**-we (*masculine*) **nosotras**-we (*feminine*)
tú-you (*familiar*)	**ustedes (Uds.)**-you (*plural*)
usted (Ud.)-you (*formal*)	**ustedes (Uds.)**-you (*plural*)
él-he	**ellos**-they (*masculine*)
ella-she	**ellas**- they (*feminine*)

- *Tú* is used when the relationship is close enough so that you could call the person by the first name.
- *Ud.* is used in any situation in which you would call the person by last name.
- *Nosotros* and *ellos* are used for a group of men or a group of men and women together.
- *Nosotras* and *ellas* are used only when the group is completely female.
- In Spain the plural of *tú* is "*vosotros*" or "*vosotras.*" "*Vosotros*" and "*vosotras*" are not used in Latin American Spanish. This workbook will not include them. In Latin America the plural of *tú* is *Uds*.

A. Translate.

1. él _____ 2. yo _____

3. nosotros _____ 4. ellos _____

5. Ud. _____ 6. nosotras _____

7. ellas _____ 8. tú _____

9. Uds. _____ 10. ella _____

B. Match the letters with the numbers.

1. yo _____	**a**. *you* (plural)
2. tú _____	**b**. *we* (masculine)
3. Ud. _____	**c**. *they* (completely feminine)
4. él_____	**ch**. *I*
5. ella_____	**d**. *they* (masculine or mixed)
6. nosotros _____	**e**. *you* (formal)
7. nosotras_____	**f**. *he*
8. Uds._____	**g**. *we* (completely feminine)
9. ellos_____	**h**. *you* (familiar)
10. ellas _____	**i**. *she*

C. What subject pronoun would you use to talk **to** the following people?

1. your brother _____
2. your Spanish professor _____
3. three of your classmates _____
4. your dog _____
5. your cousins _____
6. a child and her dad _____
7. your doctor _____
8. your best friend_____

D. What subject pronoun would you use to talk **about** the following people?

1. your friend Mary_____
2. Linda and Jack _____
3. Conchita and Francisca _____
4. President Clinton _____
5. you and your brothers_____
6. your French and Math teachers _____
7. yourself_____
8. you and your dad _____

Subject Pronouns

E. Review. Translate.

1. they (*masc.*)_____

2. I_____

3. she_____

4. you (*form.*) _____

5. he_____

6. you (*fam.*) _____

7. we (*masc.*)_____

8. they (*fem.*) _____

9. you (*pl.*)_____

10. we (*fem.*) _____

NOTE: *Check your answers in the back. If you did not get them all right, restudy the subject pronouns and then do exercise* F.

F. Review. Translate.

1. you (*form.*) _____

2. he _____

3. you (*pl.*) _____

4. we (*masc.* or *mixed*) _____

5. they (*fem.*) _____

6. I _____

7. she _____

8. you (*fam.*) _____

9. we (*fem.*) _____

10. they (*masc.* or *mixed*) _____

Subject Pronouns

Subject Pronouns

4 PRESENT TENSE OF -*AR* VERBS

- Spanish verbs have two parts: the stem (*la raíz*) (in this example, **cant**), which usually does not change, and the personal ending (*la terminación personal*) (**o, as, a, amos,** and **an**), which changes to match the pronoun you are using.

cantar to sing	
Singular	**Plural**
yo cant**o** *I sing*	nosotros-as cant**amos** *we sing*
tú cant**as** *you sing*	ustedes (Uds.) cant**an** *you sing*
usted (Ud.) cant**a** *you sing*	ustedes (Uds.) cant**an** *you sing*
él cant**a** *he sings*	ellos cant**an** *they sing*
ella cant**a** *she sings*	ellas cant**an** *they sing*

- The infinitive (*el infinitivo*) of the verb ends in **-ar, -er,** or **-ir.** In this chapter you'll be studying **-ar** verbs only.
  Here are some infinitives:

bailar	*to dance*	**estudiar**	*to study*
hablar	*to speak*	**trabajar**	*to work*

- To form the present tense (*el tiempo presente*), drop -**ar** from the infinitive and add the personal endings. Study the verb forms for the -*AR* verbs. When you think you know them very well, do the exercises.

A. Write the correct form of the subject pronoun.

  example: <u>YO</u> cant**o**

  1. _____ estudi**o** 2._____ trabaj**as** 3._____, _____, _____ cant**a** 4._____ bail**amos** 5._____, _____, _____ busc**an** 6._____ enseñ**o** 7._____ pronunci**amos** 8._____ habl**as** 9._____, _____, _____ necesit**a** 10._____ pag**amos** 11._____, _____, _____ practic**an** 12._____ regres**o** 13. _____ tom**as**

14._____, _____, _____ trabaja

15._____, _____, _____ bail**an**

16._____ busc**amos**

B. Complete the verbs with the appropriate ending.
    example: Yo habl**o**

1. Yo cant___ 2. Uds. bail_____ 3. Nosotros busc_____ 4. Ellos pag_____ 5. Tú regres_____ 6. Él trabaj_____ 7. Ellas practic_____ 8. Nosotros dese_____

C. Give the correct form of the verb. (Remember to take out -**ar** and add the appropriate ending).
    example: nosotros- hablar- habl- habl**amos**

 1. yo- cantar _____ 2. él- bailar _____

 3. ellos- trabajar _____ 4. tú -pagar _____

 5. Uds.-enseñar _____ 6. ella-estudiar _____

 7. nosotros- comprar _____ 8. Ud.- tomar _____

D. Translate. (Remember that the verb ending for *Ud.*, *él*, and *ella* is the same. The meanings are, however, different).

 1. Ud. habla _____ 2. Él habla _____

 3. Ella habla _____ 4. Ud. estudia _____

 5. Él pronuncia _____ 6. Ella pronuncia _____

 7. Él practica _____ 8. Ud. practica _____

 9. Ella compra _____ 10. Él trabaja _____

E. Make the changes following the model and translate. (Note that the verb endings remain the same because the subjects—Linda (ella), María (ella), Pedro (él), Luis (él)— are the same).
    example: Linda habla. *Ella habla.* <u>She speaks.</u>

 1. Linda estudia. _____

 2. María practica. _____

 3. Francisca pronuncia. _____

 4. La profesora compra. _____

 5. Baryshnikov baila. _____

 6. Francisco desea. _____

 7. Pedro paga. _____

8. El doctor regresa. _____

9. Conchita necesita. _____

10. El presidente enseña. _____

F. Translate. (Note that *Uds., ellos, ellas*, use the same verb endings. **However**, their meanings are different. *Uds.*= <u>you</u> (pl.); *ellos & ellas*= <u>they</u> (masculine and feminine respectively).

1. Uds. hablan _____ 2. Ellas hablan _____

3. Ellos hablan _____ 4. Uds. practican _____

5. Ellas estudian _____ 6. Uds. pronuncian _____

7. Ellos cantan _____ 8. Uds. buscan _____

9. Ellos regresan _____ 10. Ellos toman _____

G. Make the changes following the model and translate. (Note that the verb endings remain the same because the subjects—Linda y María (ellas), Pedro y Luis (ellos)— are the same.

    example: Los profesores hablan. *Ellos hablan.*

                              <u>They speak.</u> <u>They are speaking.</u>

1. Las señoritas hablan._____

2. Las profesoras bailan. _____

3. Las señoritas trabajan. _____

4. Las doctoras toman. _____

5. María y Linda regresan. _____

6. Francisca y Linda estudian. _____

7. Gloria Estefan y Julio Iglesias cantan. _____

8. Los profesores compran. _____

9. Los doctores necesitan._____

10. Pedro y María pagan. _____

H. Change following the model. (Note that anytime you add a subject to **yo**, the equivalent subject is **nosotros** and the verb will end accordingly).

    example: Luisa y yo (cantar). *Luisa y yo cantamos.*

1. Linda y yo (estudiar). _____

2. Francisco y yo (practicar). _____

3. María y yo (pronunciar)._____

4. La doctora y yo (bailar). _____

5. Los profesores y yo (trabajar). _____

Present Tense of -Ar Verbs

6. Ud. y yo (buscar). _____

7. Tú y yo (pagar). _____

8. Uds. y yo (necesitar). _____

9. Ella y yo (enseñar). _____

10. Ellos y yo (tomar). _____

I. Change following the model. Note that when you have a combined subject that includes **Ud.** or **tú**, the equivalent subject is always **Uds.** The verb will therefore end accordingly. (The exception to this is the presence of **yo.** Remember that when **yo** is part of a combined subject, the equivalent is always **nosotros.** See exercise **H.**)

example: Francisco y Ud. (estudiar). *Francisco y Ud. estudian.*

1. Las profesoras y Ud. (tomar). _____

2. Pedro y Ud. (practicar). _____

3. Ella y Ud. (cantar). _____

4. El doctor y Ud. (necesitar). _____

5. Linda y tú (hablar). _____

6. María y tú (desear). _____

7. El secretario y Ud. (comprar). _____

8. La señorita y tú (bailar). _____

9. Conchita y Ud. (trabajar). _____

10. Los estudiantes y tú (pagar). _____

J. Review. Write the subject pronoun and then translate.

example: __YO__ canto I SING (I AM SINGING)

1. _____ estudio _____

2. _____ trabajas _____

3. _____ desea _____

_____

_____

4. _____ bailamos _____

5. _____ buscan _____

_____

_____

6. _____ enseño _____

7. _____ hablas _____

Present Tense of -Ar Verbs

8. _____ necesita _____

_____

_____

9. _____ pagamos _____

10. _____ practican _____

_____

_____

11. _____ regreso _____

12. _____ tomas _____

13. _____ trabaja _____

_____

_____

14. _____ bailan _____

_____

_____

15. _____ buscamos _____

K. Review. Conjugate the verb.

1. hablar-Luis _____

2. desear-nosotros _____

3. necesitar- ellos _____

4. pagar-yo _____

5. trabajar-Uds. _____

6. tomar-el secretario y yo _____

7. enseñar-tú _____

8. bailar-María y Ud. _____

9. buscar- ella _____

10. practicar-los doctores y tú _____

Using the infinitive

- As in English, the infinitive (*el infinitivo*) is often used after another verb.
  Yo necesito trabajar en la tarde. *I need to work in the afternoon.*
- The infinitive is also used with impersonal expressions such as **es importante, es posible, es imposible,** etc.
  Es importante estudiar. *It's important to study.*

Present Tense of -Ar Verbs

L. Review. Translate. Remember that the English present progressive is translated in Spanish with the regular present tense—I am speaking= *Yo hablo*; We are singing= *Nosotros cantamos*).

1. The teacher speaks French.

_____

2. The students are studying.

_____

3. Frank and I are practicing.

_____

4. Are you (*fam.*) working?

_____

5. I need to pay.

_____

6. Julio Iglesias doesn't sing very well.

_____

7. We dance at the party.

_____

8. They (*fem.*) are returning home.

_____

9. You (*pl.*) drink coffee in the morning.

_____

10. Pedro teaches in the afternoon.

_____

11. I don't wish to return to the university.

_____

12. We are looking for the laboratory.

_____

TIPS

1. Remember that native speakers do not express subject pronouns except for emphasis or contrast.
2. In speaking, you may wish to use the subject pronouns. Thus if you somehow do not use the correct verb-ending, the presence of the subject pronoun will help you to communicate.

5 ESTAR

ESTAR-to be
yo **estoy**
tú **estás**
Ud. **está**
él, ella **está**
nosotros-as **estamos**
Uds. **están**
ellos, ellas **están**

A. Add the correct form of the subject pronoun **yo**, **tú**, **él**, **ella**, **Ud.**, **nosotros**, **nosotras**, **Uds.**, **ellos**, or **ellas**.

1. ¿_____ estoy casa?

2. _____ estamos bien.

3. ¿Cómo estás _____ ?

4. (*You pl.*) _____ están cansados.

5. (*They f.*) _____ están en el laboratorio.

6. (*They m.*)_____ están en clase.

7. (*You form.*) _____ está nervioso.

8. (*He*) _____ está en su trabajo.

B. Add the correct form of **estar**.

1. Nosotras _____ en casa.

2. (*You pl.*) _____ furiosos.

3. (*They f.*) _____ en la cafetería.

4. ¿Cómo _____ Ud.?

5. (*They m.*)_____ en la clase de geografía.

6. Ella _____ bien.

7. (*You fam.*) _____ cansado.

8. San Francisco _____ en California.

- Both **ser** and **estar** translate as *to be*. This chapter deals only with **estar**. **Ser** is covered in the next chapter. The contrast between **ser** and **estar** is explained in chapter 17.

- **Estar** means *to be*, but it can also be translated into English as *to feel, be located, taste, look, appear*, etc.

- ## Use estar

1. to indicate health:

> *Estoy bien*. I feel fine.
> *Ella está enferma*. She is sick.

2. to indicate location or position:

> *Santa Bárbara está en la costa central de California.*
> Santa Barbara is located on the central coast of California.
> *Estamos en la clase ahora*. We are in the class now.

3. with adjectives describing a temporary condition, mood or behavior such as **cansado** (tired), **contento, alegre** (happy), **cerrado** (closed), **abierto** (open), **lleno** (full), **triste** (sad), **vacío** (empty), **dormido** (sleepy), **furioso** (furious), **nervioso** (nervous), **aburrido** (bored), **preocupado** (worried), **sucio** (dirty), **limpio** (clean).

> *Esta sopa está fría*. This soup is (tastes) cold.
> *Estas enchiladas están terribles.*
> These enchiladas are (taste) terrible.
> *La puerta está cerrada*. The door is closed.
> *Los alumnos están sentados*. Students are seated.
> *Ellas están contentas ahora*. They are happy now.

4. with a number of expressions:

> *¿Está bien?* Is it O.K.?
> *Estamos de acuerdo*. We are in agreement, we agree.
> *Está claro*. It's clear.
> *Está de moda*. It's in style.

C. Fill in the correct form of **estar**. In this exercise, you will be working with the conjugation of **estar**. However, as you fill in the blanks, pay close attention to the sentences, and think about why you are using **estar**.

1. El profesor _____ ocupado ahora.
2. Los estudiantes _____ nerviosos porque hay un examen.
3. Madrid _____ en España.
4. Nosotros no _____ muy bien.
5. ¿Comprenden todo? ¿ _____ claro?
6. Mi mamá _____ contenta.
7. La enchilada _____ fría.
8. El hospital no _____ cerrado los domingos.
9. Los viernes por la noche Luis y yo _____ en las discotecas.
10. Bill Gates no _____ de acuerdo con las ideas de Karl Marx.
11. Las bibliotecas _____ abiertas los martes.
12. La minifalda _____ de moda.
13. Trabajo mucho y por eso _____ muy cansado.
14. La pizza de *Arnoldi's* no _____ deliciosa hoy.
15. La cerveza _____ en el refrigerador.

D. Review. Translate.

1. Professor Hernández is in the office.

_____

2. We don't feel fine.

_____

3. The taco tastes delicious.

_____

4. Where are you (*fam.*) at 10:00 a.m.?

_____

5. Is it clear?

_____

6. They (*masc.*) are nervous because (*porque*) they have a math exam.

_____

7. He is not busy now.

_____

8. Guadalajara is located in Mexico.

_____

9. I am seated next to (*al lado de*) María.

_____

10. The miniskirt is not in style.

_____

11. Luisa does not agree with the Spanish instructor.

_____

12. Is the library open or closed on Saturdays?

_____

13. My grand-father is tired in the afternoon.

_____

14. I am bored.

_____

15. How are you (*fam.*) doing?

_____

6 SER

SER-to be
yo **soy**
tú **eres**
Ud. **es**
él, ella **es**
nosotros-as **somos**
Uds. **son**
ellos, ellas **son**

A. Add the correct form of the subject pronoun **yo**, **tú**, **él**, **ella**, **Ud.**, **nosotros**, **nosotras**, **Uds.**, **ellos**, or **ellas.**

1. _____ somos inteligentes.

2. _____ soy baja.

3. ¿Cómo eres _____ ?

4. (*You pl.*) _____ son de Chile.

5. (*You fam.*) _____ eres arquitecto.

6. (*They m.*)_____ son mis padres.

7. (*You form.*) _____ es una buena profesora.

8. (*He*) _____ es responsable.

B. Add the correct form of **ser**.

1. Nueva York no _____ la capital de California.

2. Tú _____ estudiante.

3. Ella _____ mi abuela.

4. Ellos _____ cómicos.

5. ¿Cómo _____ Ud.?

6. Ellas _____ doctoras.

7. Uds. _____ de España.

8. Nosotras _____ las hermanas de Luis.

- In the previous chapter you learned about **estar**. This chapter deals only with **ser**. The contrast between **ser** and **estar** is explained in chapter 17.

• Use Ser

1. with adjectives to describe the normal, typical, inherent characteristic or attributes of a noun. Although these attributes are true in the mind of the speaker, i.e., how something *really* is, or someone *really* is, other people may or may not accept them as such:

> *Michael Jordan es alto.* Michael Jordan is tall.
>
> *Einstein es inteligente.* Einstein is intelligent.
>
> *La chaqueta es roja.* The jacket is red.
>
> *Mi esposo es guapo.* My husband is handsome.

2. with professions:

> *Madonna es cantante.* Madonna is a* singer.
>
> *El Señor Gómez es profesor.* Mr. Gómez is a professor.
>
> *Jack es carpintero.* Jack is a carpenter.

3. with **de** to express origin, possession, close relationships, or the material something is made of:

> *Luis es de México.* Luis is from Mexico.
>
> *Es la casa de Linda.* It's Linda's house.
>
> *El libro es de papel.* The book is made of paper.

4. to tell time:

> *Son las once.* It's eleven o'clock.

5. with **para** to tell for whom something is intended:

> *Los regalos son para los niños.* The gifts are for the children.

6. to form general statements:

> *Es necesario estudiar.* It's necessary to study.**
>
> *Es importante comer todos los días.* It's necessary to eat every day.

---

* Indefinite articles with professions (a, an) are not expressed in Spanish. If the noun is modified, however, then the indefinite article is translated. *Francisca es una excelente doctora.*

** The Spanish word for "it" as subject is "ello." However, it is almost never expressed.

C. Fill in the correct form of **ser**. In this exercise, you will be working with the conjugation of **ser**. However, as you fill in the blanks, pay close attention to the sentences, and think about why you are using **ser**.

1. Julio Iglesias _____ cantante.
2. Estos regalos no _____ para la señorita.
3. Los abuelos _____ viejos.
4. Nosotros _____ pobres.
5. _____ las ocho de la mañana.
6. Plácido Domingo _____ de España.
7. Caracas _____ la capital de Venezuela.
8. La silla _____ de metal.
9. ¿Phyllis Diller _____ bonita?
10. No _____ posible beber tequila en la clase.
11. _____ imposible jugar al fútbol en el laboratorio.
12. María _____ la hija de Pedro.
13. _____ el perro de Dolores.
14. Mis padres _____ profesores.
15. _____ las once de la noche.

D. Review. Translate.

1. I am from Barcelona.

_____

2. Students are responsible.

_____

3. The car is not old.

_____

4. This beer is for Pancho.

_____

5. What's this?

_____

6. It's ten p.m.

_____

7. The table is made of wood (*madera*).

_____

8. Luisa is a doctor.

_____

9. It's not practical to watch television twelve hours a day.

_____

10. Where are you (*form.*) from?

_____

11. They are good friends.

_____

12. My parents are not rich.

_____

13. It's Linda's car.

_____

14. Los Angeles is not the capital of California.

_____

15. My sister wants (*quiere*) to be a psychologist (*sicóloga*).

_____

7 DESCRIPTIVE ADJECTIVES

Agreement

- Descriptive adjectives (*los adjetivos calificativos*) agree in gender and number with the noun they describe.
- Adjectives ending in "**o**" in the masculine have four forms: **-o,-a,-os,-as.**

	masculine	feminine
singular:	el hombre alt**o**	la mujer alt**a**
plural :	los hombres alt**os**	las mujeres alt**as**

- Adjectives ending in "**e**" or a **consonant** have two forms, one for the singular, the other for the plural: **-e, -consonant,** and **es**

el libro verd**e**	la mesa verd**e**
los libros verd**es**	las mesas verd**es**
el hombre formal	la mujer formal
los hombres formal**es**	las mujeres formal**es**

- Adjectives ending in "**és**" in the masculine have four forms as follows:

  francés-franceses

  francesa-francesas

  Common adjectives following this pattern include *portugués, inglés, holandés* (Dutch), *japonés, danés* (Danish), *irlandés* (Irish) etc.

A. Change from singular to plural.

1. el chico alto _____

2. la mujer rica _____

3. el paciente sentimental _____

4. la doctora inteligente_____

5. el coche verde _____

6. la casa vieja _____

7. el joven francés _____

8. la ciudad holandesa _____

9. el doctor trabajador _____

10. la señorita japonesa _____

11. el restaurante inglés _____

12. el cliente irlandés _____

B. Circle the adjectives (*los adjetivos*) that could be used to describe the noun without changing forms.

1. la dependienta (alta, rubio, danesa, formal, mexicana, conservador, fiel)
2. los amigos (portugués, morenos, viejas, casados, jóvenes, intelectual)
3. la casa (grande, interesante, fascinante, nuevo, feas, gris, azul)
4. la excursión (importante, barato, excelente, terrible, italiano)
5. el carro (francesa, nuevo, caro, verde, barata)
6. las discusiones (largas, formales, serios, demócraticas)

Position of Adjectives

- Most adjectives are placed **after** the noun:

  el coche italiano the Italian car

  la casa verde the green house

  las señoras mexicanas the Mexican ladies

  los tacos deliciosos the delicious tacos

- Not all adjectives are placed after the noun. Adjectives describing one-of-a-kind nouns come **before** the noun.

  su artística esposa his artistic wife (he only has one wife; "*su esposa artística*" suggests he has another wife who is not artistic)

  la antigua ciudad de Cuzco the ancient city of Cuzco (There is only one Cuzco).

- When an adjective describes an intrinsic, or typical, quality of the noun, it is placed **before** the noun.

  la blanca nieve (Snow is almost always white; "*la nieve blanca*" suggests that some snow may be whiter than others: *Me gusta la nieve blanca, no me gusta la nieve sucia.* I like the white snow, I don't like dirty snow.)

  los verdes pinos the green pines

  las altas montañas the high mountains

- The adjectives *bueno* and *malo* may either follow or precede the noun. When they precede it, they usually suggest an emphasis in the mind of the speaker:

  una buena doctora a good doctor

  una mala ciudad a bad city

un mal* profesor a bad teacher

un buen restaurante a good restaurant

- *grande, pobre, viejo, nuevo* can precede or follow the noun. Changing where you put the adjective will change the meaning of the words:
- *Un diccionario es un libro **grande**.* A dictionary is a **big** book.

  *Don Quijote de la Mancha es un **gran**** libro. Don Quijote de La Mancha* is a **great** book.
- *Ellos viven en una casa grande.* They live in a big house.

  Ellas viven en una gran casa. They live in a great house.
- *Yo necesito un coche nuevo.* I need a new car (brand new).

  Yo manejo un nuevo coche. I am driving a different car.
- *Es un pobre señor.* He is a poor, unfortunate man.

  Es un señor pobre. He is a poor (not rich) man
- *Es una vieja amiga.* She is an old friend, long-standing.

  Es una amiga vieja. She is an elderly friend.

C. Place the adjective (*el adjetivo*) before or after the noun.

1. un _____ hombre _____ (alto)

2. una _____ doctora _____ (rica)

3. un _____ paciente _____ (amable)

4. el _____ alumno _____ (pobre, *not rich*)

5. la _____ chica _____ (inteligente)

6. una _____ clase _____ (grande, large)

7. la _____ señorita _____ (alemana)

8. la _____ lección _____ (larga)

9. el _____ lápiz _____ (rojo)

10. un _____ secretario _____ (impaciente)

11. la _____ ciudad _____ (gran)

12. el _____ presidente _____ (gran)

13. una _____ enchilada _____ (deliciosa)

14. el _____ amigo _____ (buen)

---

* "bueno" and "malo" drop the "o" when they precede the noun.

** When "grande" precedes the noun, it drops "de" in its masculine and feminine singular forms. In these cases, in addition to "great", its meaning can be "impressive," or "famous."
    But: *una gran parte*- a big part

15. el _____ edificio _____ (bueno)
16. la _____ silla _____ (cómoda)
17. un _____ diccionario _____ (completo)
18. un _____ turista _____ (pobre, *unfortunate*)
19. la _____ ciudad de París _____ (hermosa)
20. la _____ ciudad de Sisquoc _____ (pequeña)
21. el _____ amigo _____ (viejo, *age*)
22. la _____ parte _____ (gran)
23. una _____ bicicleta _____ (nueva)
24. su _____ esposo _____ (guapo)

D. Review. Change from singular to plural.

1. el libro viejo _____
2. la señora rica _____
3. el doctor inglés _____
4. la cliente holandesa _____
5. la lección larga _____
6. el chico trabajador _____

E. Review. Place a check mark next to the correct responses.

1. el taco delicioso _____

2. el delicioso taco _____

3. la ciudad grande (*great city*) _____

4. la gran ciudad (*great city*) _____

5. su esposa inteligente _____

6. su inteligente esposa _____

7. unos jóvenes amables _____

8. unos amables jóvenes _____

9. la mujer pobre (*unfortunate*) _____

10. la pobre mujer (*unfortunate*) _____

F. Review. Translate.

1. an interesting class _____

2. the green pines _____

3. the bad doctor _____

4. a comfortable chair _____

5. a small elephant _____

6. a great man _____

7. an old friend (*masc., long-standing*) _____

8. her handsome husband _____

8 PRESENT TENSE OF -ER & -IR VERBS

Study the verb forms for the -ER and -IR verbs. When you think you know them very well, do the exercises.

COMER		ESCRIBIR	
singular	plural	singular	plural
yo como	nosotros comemos	yo escribo	nosotros escribimos
tú comes	Uds. comen	tú escribes	Uds. escriben
Ud. come	Uds. comen	Ud. escribe	Uds. escriben
él come	ellos comen	él escribe	ellos escriben
ella come	ellas comen	ella escribe	ellas escriben

Note that the only difference between the endings for these two groups is in the *nosotros* form: with -ER the ending is -emos; with -IR it's -imos.

A. Write the correct form of the subject pronoun.

    example: __YO__ leo.

1. _____ vendo 2. _____ vives 3. _____, _____,

_____ escribe 4. _____ creemos 5. _____, _____

_____beben 6. _____ escribo 7. _____ aprendemos

8. _____ asistes 9. _____, _____, _____ vive

10. _____ insistimos

B. Complete the verbs with the appropriate ending.

    example: Yo aprend**o**

1. Yo beb ___ 2. Uds. com _____ 3. Nosotros comprend_____ 4. Ellos

cre _____ 5. Tú deb _____ 6. Él le _____ 7. Ellas vend _____

8. Nosotros abr_____ 9. Uds. asist _____

10. Yo escrib _____

C. Give the correct form of the verb. (Remember to take out -**er** or -**ir** and add the appropriate ending).

      example: nosotros- comer— com—com**emos**

1. yo- vender _____
2. él- abrir _____
3. ellos- aprender _____
4. tú - beber _____
5. Uds.- comprender _____
6. ella- asistir _____
7. nosotros- recibir _____
8. Ud.- insistir _____
9. yo- creer _____
10. él- vivir _____
11. ellos- deber _____
12. nosotros- comer _____
13. Uds.- vender _____
14. tú- leer _____
15. nosotros- deber _____
16. Ud.- creer _____

D. Review. Write the correct form of the subject pronoun and then translate.

      example: <u>YO</u> vivo <u>I LIVE (I AM LIVING)</u>

1. _____ abro _____
2. _____ asistes _____
3. _____ escribe _____

_____

_____

4. _____ recibimos _____
5. _____ viven _____

_____

_____

6. _____ vendo _____
7. _____ bebes _____
8. _____ come _____

_____

_____

9. _____ comprendemos _____
10. _____ creen _____

_____

_____

11. _____ debo _____
12. _____ lees _____

Present Tense of -Er and -Ir Verbs

13. _____ vende _____

_____

_____

14. _____ abrimos _____
15. _____ asisten _____

_____

_____

E. Review. Conjugate the verb.

1. vivir-Luis _____

2. aprender-nosotros _____

3. abrir- ellos_____

4. beber-yo _____

5. vender-Uds._____

6. escribir-el secretario y yo _____

7. insistir-tú_____

8. leer-María y Ud. _____

9. recibir- yo _____

10. creer-los doctores y tú _____

F. Review. Translate.

1. The teacher eats a lot.

_____

2. The students are opening the book.

_____

3. Frank and I are reading.

_____

4. Are you (*fam.*) writing?

_____

5. I must pay.

_____

6. Children receive lots of gifts.

_____

7. We don't drink much at parties.

_____

8. They (*fem.*) are learning a lot.

_____

9. You (*pl.*) don't sell your Spanish books.

_____

10. Pedro lives in Santa Barbara.

_____

11. My daughter believes in Santa Claus.

_____

12. I don't attend classes at night.

_____

13. Does the president understand my problems?

_____

14. Some students insist on speaking English in the French class.

_____

Present Tense of -Er and -Ir Verbs

9 POSSESSIVE ADJECTIVES

mi coche	*my car*
mis coches	*my cars*
tu casa	*your house* (*fam.*)
tus casas	*your houses* (*fam.*)
su profesor	*your/his/her/their professor*
sus profesores	*your/his/her/their professors*
nuestro* padre	*our father*
nuestra madre	*our mother*
nuestros hermanos	*our brothers/our brothers and sisters*
nuestras hermanas	*our sisters*

- The possessive **su** can also mean "its." The context clarifies the multiple meanings of **su**. If not, you can use **de** and a noun to make the distinction:
  su coche or **el coche de él**; **su casa** or **la casa de ellos**, etc.
- Note that possessive adjectives (*los adjetivos posesivos*) agree with the object being possessed and not the possessor.
- The English possessive "their" translates in Spanish as **su** if followed by a singular noun or **sus** if followed by a plural one:
  su hermano=*their brother;* sus hermanos: *their brothers.*
- There is no '**s** in Spanish. It comes out with the preposition **de:**
  Mary's class: *la clase de Mary.*

A. Circle the appropriate possessive adjective (*adjetivos posesivos*).

1. Mi/mis coche es pequeño.
2. Nuestra/nuestro profesora es inteligente.
3. Su/sus blusas son bonitas.
4. ¿Tu/tus amigos hablan francés?
5. Nuestros/nuestras hermanos son perezosos.

---

* The possessives **vuestro, vuestra, vuestros, vuestras** (your, familiar plural) are used only in Spain. This Workbook will not include them.

B. Change from singular to plural.

1. su gato _____   4. nuestro libro _____
2. nuestra casa _____   5. su doctora _____
3. tu mesa_____   6. mi perro_____

C. Fill in the appropriate possessive adjective (*los adjetivos posesivos*). The underlined subject is a clue as to which possessive you should use.

1. Yo hablo español con _____ profesora de español. Hablo inglés con _____ otros profesores.
2. Luis habla inglés con _____ hermano, pero habla italiano con _____ primos.
3. Nosotras hablamos con _____ padre en casa. Hablamos por teléfono con _____ primos argentinos.
4. Tú hablas alemán con _____ amigos austriacos. Hablas inglés con _____ mamá.
5. Ellos hablan con _____ profesor de matemáticas en la universidad. Hablan con _____ perros en el jardín.
6. ¿Ud. habla con _____ gato en español o en francés?

D. Review. Translate.

1. my friends _____
2. your shirt (*form.*) _____
3. her father _____
4. their parents _____
5. your car (*fam.*) _____
6. our grandfather _____
7. his classes _____
8. her cats _____
9. our president _____
10. your ideas (*fam.*) _____
11. her boyfriend _____
12. his shoes _____
13. my house _____
14. their radio _____
15. his sisters _____
16. her hat _____

10 PRESENT TENSE OF *TENER, VENIR, PREFERIR, QUERER, PODER*

Study the following verbs. Pay special attention to the irregularities which are shown in bold face. After you study the verbs, do the exercises. Note that the *nosotros* forms are completely regular.

tener (to have)	venir (to come)	preferir (to prefer)	querer (to want)	poder (to be able)
tengo	vengo	prefiero	quiero	puedo
tienes	vienes	prefieres	quieres	puedes
tiene	viene	prefiere	quiere	puede
tenemos	venimos	preferimos	queremos	podemos
tienen	vienen	prefieren	quieren	pueden

A. Write the correct form of the subject pronoun and then translate.

  example: <u>YO</u> quiero. <u>I want</u>.

1. _____ vengo _____
2. _____ puedes _____
3. _____ prefiere_____
   _____
   _____
4. _____ venimos _____
5. _____ tienen _____
   _____
   _____
6. _____ puedo_____
7. _____ quieres_____
8. _____ viene _____
   _____
   _____
9. _____ preferimos _____
10. _____ tengo_____

Present tense of tener, venir, preferir, querer, poder

B. Review. Conjugate the verb.

1. poder-tú_____
2. querer-María y Ud. _____
3. poder- yo_____
4. venir-los doctores y tú _____
5. tener-Luis _____
6. poder-nosotros _____
7. querer- ellos _____
8. venir-yo_____
9. tener -Uds._____
10. preferir-el secretario y yo _____

C. Review. Translate.

1. I don't have a lot of money.

   _____

2. We want to learn French.

   _____

3. Students come to school on time.

   _____

4. Bill Clinton prefers to eat at McDonald's.

   _____

5. My father and I can play the piano.

   _____

6. The doctor cannot come to your house.

   _____

7. Julio Iglesias wants to sing in English.

   _____

8. Can you (*fam.*) eat eleven enchiladas?

   _____

9. Donald Trump and Marla Maples prefer to live in New York.

   _____

10. Imelda Marcos has lots of shoes.

   _____

Present tense of tener, venir, preferir, querer, poder

11 *IR; IR + A +* **INFINITIVE**

ir *to go*	
yo **voy** *I go, am going*	nosotros **vamos** *we go, are going*
tú **vas** *you* (fam.)*go , are going*	nosotras **vamos** *we go, are going*
Ud. **va** *you go, are going*	Uds. **van** *you* (pl.) *go, are going*
él, ella **va** *he/she goes, is going*	ellos, ellas **van** *they go, are going*

A. Add the correct form of the subject pronoun.

1. ¿_____ vas a casa?

2. _____ voy a mi trabajo.

3. _____ vamos a la escuela.

4. (*You pl.*) _____ van a un restaurante.

5. (*They f.*) _____ van a un restaurante.

6. (*They m.*)_____ van a un restaurante.

7. (*You form.*) _____ va a su clase de sociología.

8. (*He*) _____ va a su clase de sociología.

9. (*She*) _____ va a su clase de sociología.

B. Add the correct form of **ir** (*voy, vas, va, vamos, van, ir*).

1. ¿Adónde _____ Uds. a las nueve?

2. Nosotras no _____ a clase el domingo.

3. María _____ a la casa de su abuelo.

4. ¿Tú _____ a una discoteca el sábado?

5. Yo _____ a México en coche.

6. Ellos no desean _____ a Death Valley en agosto.

7. Ud. _____ a su trabajo.

8. Pancho no _____ a Santa Bárbara en autostop (*hitchiking*).

- The present of **ir** can also be used with the preposition **a** and an infinitive to translate actions in the near future (*el futuro inmediato*).
- Este fin de semana yo **voy a visitar** a mi primo.
  This week-end I am going to visit my cousin.
- El viernes nosotros **vamos a bailar** en una discoteca.
  On Friday we are going to dance in a discotheque.

C. Change from present to near future.
   modelos: Yo bailo. *Yo voy a bailar.*
          Uds. cantan. *Uds. van a cantar.*

1. Tú comes. _____

2. Nosotros practicamos. _____

3. Uds. estudian. _____

4. Luisa y yo buscamos. _____

5. Ella recibe. _____

6. Yo escribo. _____

7. Isabel compra. _____

8. Ellos bailan. _____

D. Review. Translate.

1. I don't go to school on Sundays.

_____

2. We are going to Spain.

_____

3. My dad goes to work everyday.

_____

4. Where are you (*fam.*) going?

_____

5. He is going to practice tomorrow.

_____

6. They don't want to go to the laboratory at seven a.m.

_____

7. She is going to write many letters this weekend.

_____

8. Mercedes and I are going to take a math class.

_____

12 PRESENT TENSE OF *HACER, PONER, SALIR, OÍR, TRAER,* AND *VER*

hacer *to do, make*	poner *to put, place*	salir *to leave, go out*
hago	pongo	salgo
haces	pones	sales
hace	pone	sale
hacemos	ponemos	salimos
hacen	ponen	salen

A. Write the correct form of the subject pronoun and then translate.
   example: <u>YO</u> salgo. <u>I leave, go out</u>

1. _____ pongo _____

2. _____ haces _____

3. _____ sale _____

_____

_____

4. _____ ponemos _____

5. _____ salen _____

_____

_____

6. _____ hacen_____

_____ _____

_____ _____

7. _____ hago_____

8. _____ sales _____

- **Hacer** means "to do" or "to make." Questions with **hacer** are often answered with another verb.

    ¿Qué hace Ud. en una discoteca? Bailo.
    What do you do in a discotheque? I dance.
    ¿Qué hace el enfermero los lunes? Trabaja en el hospital.
    What does the nurse do on Mondays? He works in the hospital.

- **Hacer** is used in many idiomatic expressions.

    Hace frío. *It's cold.* Hace calor. *It's hot.*
    hacer ejercicio *to exercise;* hacer una pregunta *to ask a question*
    hacer un viaje *to take a trip*

- **Poner** means "to put, to place". It is also used to mean "to turn on" an appliance.

    Yo pongo crema en el café. *I put cream in coffee.*
    Ponen el estéreo. *They turn on the stereo.*

- **Salir** means "to go out, to leave." With the preposition "para" it means "to leave for."

    La profesora Little sale para Sudamérica.
    Professor Little is leaving for South America.

- With the preposition "con" it means "to go out" (on a date).

    Pancho sale con Luisa. *Pancho goes out with Luisa.*

- With the preposition "de" it means "to go out from, to leave a place."

    Isabel sale de casa a las ocho. *Isabel leaves home at eight.*

B. Write the correct form of **hacer, poner, or salir**.

1. En la clase de química yo no comprendo mucho. Entonces yo (hacer) _____ muchas preguntas.

2. Jesús (salir) _____ para España mañana.

3. Mi papá y yo no (poner) _____ azúcar en el café.

4. En la mañana María (hacer) _____ ejercicio y mira la televisión.

5. Están de vacaciones. Ellos (hacer) _____ un viaje a Europa.

6. ¿Quieres escuchar música en el coche? ¿Por qué no (poner) _____ el radio?

7. A veces nosotros (salir) _____ de clase tarde porque el profesor habla y habla y habla.

8. (Hacer) _____ mucho calor en el desierto.

oír *to hear*	traer *to bring*	ver *to see*
oigo	traigo	veo
oyes	traes	ves
oye	trae	ve
oímos	traemos	vemos
oyen	traen	ven

C. Write the correct form of the subject pronoun and then translate.

    example: <u>YO</u> veo. <u>I see</u>

1. _____ oigo _____

2. _____ traes _____

3. _____ ve _____

    _____

    _____

4. _____ oímos _____

5. _____ traen _____

    _____

    _____

6. _____ ves _____

7. _____ traigo _____

8. _____ oyen _____

    _____

    _____

- The command forms of **oír** —oye tú, oiga Ud., and oigan Uds.— are used to attract attention. They mean "listen" or "hey."

D. Write the correct form of **oír, traer,** or **ver**.

1. Cuando duermo, yo no _____ (oír) nada.

2. Nosotros _____ (ver) programas en español en la televisión.

3. ¿Tú _____ (traer) cerveza a clase?

4. Mi abuelo no _____ (ver) bien y por eso necesita lentes (*glasses*).

5. ¿Uds. _____ (oír) el ruido (*noise*?

6. Los estudiantes a veces no _____ (traer) sus libros al laboratorio.

Present tense of *hacer, poner, salir, oír, traer,* and *ver*

E. Review. Translate.

1. What do you (*fam.*) do on Friday nights?

_____

2. At what time does your (*form.*) brother leave home in the morning?

_____

3. We don't bring wine to class.

_____

4. I see very well. I don't need glasses.

_____

5. Luis turns on the radio in the afternoon.

_____

6. It's cold now.

_____

7. My grandfather doesn't hear very well.

_____

8. Sometimes we go out of the Spanish class late because the instructor *fem.*) talks too much.

_____

9. When students don't understand something (*algo*), they ask questions.

_____

10. Do you (*pl.*) bring pens or pencils for your exams?

_____

11. Does your (*fam.*) dad put cream in his coffee?

_____

12. I can't hear very well now.

_____

Present tense of *hacer, poner, salir, oír, traer,* and *ver*

13 PRESENT TENSE OF STEM-CHANGING VERBS

Study the forms for the stem-changing verbs (*los verbos que cambian la raíz*). When you think you know them very well, do the exercises.

E>IE

pensar (ie)
to think, to intend, to plan
yo pienso
tú piensas
Ud. piensa
él, ella piensa
nosotros pensamos
Uds. piensan
ellos, ellas piensan

- Other verbs that make the stem change from "e" to "ie" include:
cerrar (to close), *empezar* (to begin), *entender* (to understand), and *perder* (to lose).

- Remember that the *nosotros* form does not make a stem change.

A. Write the correct form of the verb.

1. Yo (cerrar) _____ la puerta.
2. Luisa (empezar) _____ la lección.
3. Tú (entender) _____ todo.
4. Nosotros (pensar) _____ ir a México en el futuro.
5. Uds. (perder) _____ mucho dinero en Las Vegas.
6. Nosotros (cerrar) _____ las ventanas.
7. Los chicos (empezar) _____ el examen.
8. Los doctores (entender)_____ español.
9. Mi padre siempre (perder) _____ sus llaves (keys).
10. El profesor (pensar) _____ en sus problemas.

O>UE

volver (ue) *to return*
yo **vue**lvo
tú **vue**lves
Ud. **vue**lve
él, ella **vue**lve
nosotros volvemos
Uds. **vue**lven
ellos, ellas **vue**lven

- Other verbs that make the stem change from "**o**" to "**ue**" include *almorzar* (to have lunch), *dormir* (to sleep), and *jugar* (to play).
- Remember that the *nosotros* form does not make a stem change.

B. Write the correct form of the verb.
1. Tú (volver) _____ aquí mañana.
2. Conchita (almorzar) _____ en su coche.
3. Nosotros (dormir) _____ en la clase de matemáticas.
4. Ud. y su hermano (jugar) _____ a la lotería.
5. Yo (volver) _____a casa muy tarde.
6. Mis amigos (dormir) _____ muchas horas.
7. Los turistas (almorzar) _____ en el restaurante.
8. Michael Jordan no (jugar) _____ bien al fútbol.

E>I

pedir (i) *to ask for, to order*
yo pido
tú pides
Ud., él, ella pide
él, ella pide
nosotros pedimos
Uds. piden
ellos, ellas piden

Present Tense of Stem-Changing Verbs

Other verbs that make the stem change from "e" to "i" include *servir* (to serve), *repetir* (to repeat), and *seguir* * (to follow).

C. Write the correct form of the verb.

1. Tú (repetir) _____ las palabras de la profesora.
2. Conchita (pedir) _____ cerveza en el bar.
3. Nosotros (seguir) _____ las instrucciones.
4. Ud. y su hermano (servir) _____ vino en la fiesta.
5. Yo no (pedir) _____muchos favores.
6. Mis amigos (seguir) _____ a las chicas.
7. Los estudiantes (repetir) _____ en el laboratorio.
8. Luis y yo (servir)_____ comida francesa.

D. Review. Translate.

1. We have lunch at one.

_____

2. Some students are thinking about going (*ir*) to Europe in the future.

_____

3. The Spanish teacher is beginning to lose his patience (paciencia).

_____

4. Pedro always orders tacos and enchiladas.

_____

5. I never serve wine at my parties.

_____

6. When are you (*form.*) returning home?

_____

7. Do you understand (*fam.*) the lesson?

_____

---

* The *yo* form of *seguir* is *sigo*.

Present Tense of Stem-Changing Verbs

8. My wife always loses money when she plays the lottery.

_____

9. The students are beginning to understand Spanish.

_____

10. My elephant sleeps ten hours a day.

_____

11. The students repeat the new words.

_____

12. The girls are following the boys.

_____

14 REFLEXIVE VERBS

Reflexive Verbs in English

Reflexive verbs (*los verbos reflexivos*) must be used with a reflexive pronoun. In English the pronouns are *-self* and *-selves*. In a reflexive verb the action goes back to the subject, i.e., hence the reflection.

I dress myself. They buy themselves a new car.

Many English verbs used to describe our daily routine—*to get up, to go to bed, to shave, to get dressed*, etc., are translated in Spanish with reflexive verbs.

Reflexive Pronouns in Spanish

me-myself	*nos*-ourselves
te-yourself (*familiar*)	*se*-yourselves
se-yourself (*formal*) *se*-himself, herself, itself	*se*-themselves

lavarse (to wash oneself)

yo me lavo-I wash myself	*nosotros nos lavamos*-we wash ourselves
tú te lavas-you wash yourself *Ud. se lava*- you wash yourself	*Uds. se lavan*-you wash yourselves *Uds. se lavan*-you wash yourselves
él se lava-he washes himself *ella se lava*-she washes herself	*ellos se lavan*-they wash themselves *ellas se lavan*-they wash themselves

The following are the most common reflexive verbs in Spanish

acostarse (ue)-to go to bed	*ponerse*-to put something on
afeitarse-to shave	*quedarse*-to stay
bañarse-to take a bath	*quitarse*-to take off
despertarse (ie)-to wake up	*sentarse (ie)*-to sit down
divertirse (ie)-to have a good time	*vestirse (i)*-to get dressed
ducharse-to take a shower	*maquillarse*-to put make up on
lavarse-to wash oneself	*peinarse*-to comb oneself
levantarse-to get up	*dormirse (ue)*-to fall asleep

As you can see, most are -ar verbs. Some are stem-changing verbs.

> *Yo me levanto tarde.* I get up late.
>
> *Tú te bañas en la mañana.* You take a bath in the morning.
>
> *Ud. se afeita todos los días.* You shave everyday.
>
> *Luis se sienta aquí.* Luis sits here.
>
> *Nosotros nos vestimos rápidamente.* We get dressed rapidly.
>
> *Uds. se quedan hasta muy tarde.* You stay until very late.
>
> *Las chicas no se duermen en clase.* The girls do not fall asleep in class.

Position of Reflexive Pronouns

As you can easily see form the previous examples, the reflexive pronouns are placed just **before** the verb.

If an infinitive is present, the reflexive pronoun may be placed in front of the conjugated verb or may be attached to the infinitive:

- Yo no **me** quiero levantar. Yo no quiero levantar**me.**
- Los chicos **se** van a sentar aquí. Los chicos van a sentar**se** aquí.

A. Circle the correct reflexive pronoun (*el pronombre reflexivo*).

1. Tú te/se levantas tarde.
2. Nosotros me/nos acostamos temprano.
3. Yo te/me maquillo en el coche.
4. Ellos nos/se divierten.
5. Ud. me/se ducha todos los días.
6. Luisa y yo se/nos quedamos aquí hasta las dos de la tarde.
7. Tú y tu novio nos/se sientan juntos (together).
8. Francisco te/se afeita en el cuarto de baño.
9. Yo me/nos visto despacio.
10. Nosotros te/nos quitamos la chaqueta.

B. Review. Fill in the reflexive pronoun (*el pronombre reflexivo*).

1. Yo _____ despierto a las ocho.
2. Uds. _____ acuestan temprano.
3. Tú _____ duchas en casa.
4. Los chicos no _____ maquillan.
5. Pedro y yo _____ sentamos en la silla.

6. Ellos no pueden sentar _____ allí.

7. Ellos no _____ pueden sentar allí.

8. Yo no quiero levantar _____ temprano.

9. Yo no _____ quiero levantar temprano.

10. ¿_____ vas a afeitar?

11. ¿Vas a afeitar_____ ?

12. Queremos bañar_____ pronto.

13. _____ queremos bañar pronto.

14. ¿Puedes quedar _____ aquí?

15. ¿_____ puedes quedar aquí?

C. Review. Translate.

1. Linda gets up early.

_____

2. We don't shave everyday.

_____

3. They fall asleep in class.

_____

4. He takes a shower once or twice a day.

_____

5. I never put on make up in class.

_____

6. Many students sit in the front.

_____

7. Pancho prefers to sit next to Maria.

_____

8. Mercedes and you (*fam.*) stay here until five p.m.

_____

9. We get dressed in a hurry.

_____

10. I take a bath everyday.

_____

11. Carlos has a good time at my parties.

_____

12. Are you (*fam.*) going to bed soon?

_____

13. Sometimes I can't fall asleep very fast.

_____

14. My son does not want to wake up early on Sundays.

_____

15. Antonio sits next to Luisa.

_____

NOTES: *1) In the previous exercises all verbs required a reflexive pronoun because they were used reflexively, i.e., the action went back to the person doing it, hence, the reflection. Any of the verbs in the previous exercises can be used without the reflexive pronoun to mean something a little different. Compare:*

- *despertar-to wake someone up despertarse-to wake oneself up*

- *dormir-to sleep dormirse-to fall asleep*

- *poner-to put, place ponerse-to put on*

- *Yo me levanto. I get up. Yo levanto al bebé. I lift the baby.*

- *Ud. se baña. You take a bath.*

  Ud. baña al paciente. You give the patient a bath.

2) Most verbs, which are normally used without a reflexive pronoun, could be used thus if one wishes to:

  hablar-to speak/ hablarse-to speak to oneself

  escribir-to write/escribirse-to write to oneself

- *Yo hablo francés con mi profesora. I speak French with my professor.*

  Yo me hablo en francés. I speak to myself in French.

- *Luis escribe poemas. Luis writes poems.*

  Luis se escribe poemas. Luis writes himself poems.

3) Note that sometimes Spanish uses the reflexive where English uses the possessive:

- *Yo me pongo el sombrero. I put on my hat.*

- *Ella se lava la cara. She washes her face.*

- *El doctor se quita la chaqueta. The doctor takes off his jacket.*

15 DEMONSTRATIVE ADJECTIVES

singular	plural
esta casa *this house* este coche *this car*	estas casas *these houses* estos coches *these cars*
esa pluma *that pen* ese sombrero *that hat*	esas plumas *those pens* esos sombreros *those hats*
aquel chico *that boy* (over there) aquella chica *that girl* (over there)	aquellos chicos *those boys* (over there) aquellas chicas *those girls* (over there)

- Use **este, esta, estos, estas** when the items are near the speaker.

- Use **ese, esa, esos, esas** when the items are near the listener.

- Use **aquel, aquella, aquellos, aquellas** when the items are far away from both listener and speaker. In essence, the phrase "over there" is included.

- To turn these demonstrative adjectives (*adjetivos demostrativos*) into pronouns, just delete the noun and add an accent mark on the "e"—**éste, ésta, éstos, éstas, ése, ésa, ésos, ésas, aquél, aquélla, aquéllos, aquéllas**:
    esta casa y aquélla *this house and that one over there*

A. Change from singular to plural. As you do the exercise, review the meaning for yourself.

1. esta mesa _____

2. este muchacho _____

3. aquella señora _____

4. ese vestido _____

5. aquel almacén _____

6. esta estudiante _____

7. esa casa _____

8. aquella situación _____

9. ese reloj _____

10. aquella chaqueta _____

- To describe ideas, situations, concepts that cannot be classified as either masculine or feminine, use **esto, eso,** or **aquello**. These neuter forms never change.

B. React to the situations by using one the phrases at the right.

1. Ud. gana la lotería.

_____

2. Pedro está en el hospital.

_____

3. La profesora de matemáticas cancela el examen final.

_____

4. Ud. no tiene gasolina en su coche y no tiene dinero.

_____

5. Ud. y sus amigos están en una fiesta.

_____

6. Ud. saca una "A" en el examen de español.

_____

a. Eso es terrible.

b. Eso es magnífico.

C. Review. Translate.

1. that dress _____
2. those boys (*over there*) _____
3. this car and that one _____
4. That's terrible. _____
5. that situation _____
6. these stories _____
7. that house (*over there*) _____
8. That's great. _____
9. these watches _____
10. this shirt _____
11. those exams _____
12. that knapsack _____

Demonstrative Adjectives

16 PRESENT PROGRESSIVE

yo estoy estudiando *I am studying*
tú estás estudiando *you are studying*
Ud. está estudiando *you are studying*
él/ella está estudiando *he/she is studying*
nosotros/nosotras estamos estudiando *we are studying*
Uds. están estudiando *you are studying*
ellos/ellas están estudiando *they are studying*

- To form the present progressive, use the present of **estar** and the present participle. The present participle ends in -**ando** for -**ar** verbs and in -**iendo** for -**er** and -**ir** verbs. It always ends in -**o**.
  estudiar- estudi**ando**; comer-com**iendo**; escribir-escrib**iendo**.

- Stem-changing verbs in -**ir** retain the change in the present participle:
  servir-s**i**rviendo; pedir-p**i**diendo; repetir-rep**i**tiendo; seguir-s**i**guiendo; vestir-v**i**stiendo; dormir-d**u**rmiendo.

- Verbs in -**ar** and -**er** don't make a stem change in the present participle: pensar-*pensando*; volver-*volviendo*.

- Spanish uses the present progressive (*el presente progresivo*) to express an action in progress (right now). In English, the present progressive may also mean a future or a habitual action. These cases are given in Spanish as regular present tenses.
  They are calling tomorrow. Ellos llaman mañana.
  He is studying French this year. Él estudia francés este año.

- Spelling changes: some verbs change the **i** to **y** in the present participle: leer-leyendo; traer-trayendo; ir-yendo; oír-oyendo.

A. Give the present participle (*el gerundio*).
   examples: cantar-*cantando*; salir-*saliendo*

1. bailar _____
2. mirar _____
3. comer _____
4. leer _____
5. vivir_____

6. traer _____
7. servir _____
8. perder _____
9. hacer _____
10. aprender_____

• Reflexive pronouns may be placed before the form of **estar** or attached to the present participle. If you attach them, an accent mark is placed on the **a** or **e** before the ending -**ndo**.

Yo me estoy levantando **or** Yo estoy levantándome.

Ellas se están divirtiendo **or** Ellas están divirtiéndose.

B. Change from present to present progressive (*presente progresivo*).
example: yo canto- *yo estoy cantando*

1. Linda fuma. _____

2. Nosotras jugamos. _____

3. Tú haces. _____

4. Ellos llegan. _____

5. Yo me levanto. _____

6. Pancho y Mercedes trabajan. _____

7. Él sale. _____

8. Nosotros vivimos. _____

9. Ellas traen. _____

10. Tú sirves. _____

11. Yo recibo. _____

12. Ud. se viste. _____

13. Francisco vende. _____

14. Nosotros pedimos. _____

15. Yo oigo. _____

C. Review. Translate. Use the present progressive where appropriate.

1. I normally eat at home, but now I am eating in a restaurant.

_____

2. They usually study in the library, but now they are studying in their car.

_____

Present Progressive

3. Pedro plays soccer on Fridays, but now he is playing tennis.

_____

4. We generally watch television at night, but now we are reading.

_____

5. Isabel dances on Saturday nights, but now she is doing her homework.

_____

6. Are you (*fam.*) smoking right now?

_____

7. They are getting up right now.

_____

8. I am not ordering pizza now, but I am going to order pizza later.

_____

9. What are you (*form.*) doing right now?

_____

10. Are students thinking in English or in Spanish right now?

_____

11. We are not taking a shower right now.

_____

12. She is not listening to the radio right now.

_____

17 SER Vs. ESTAR

- In chapters 5 and 6 you learned the forms and usage of **estar** and **ser**. Both can translate in English as *to be,* but **estar** is often expressed as *to feel, look, appear, taste,* etc.

- Remember that, in general, **ser** expresses a reality that is considered inherent, true, and real by the speaker and quite likely everybody would accept as truthful. This reality need not necessarily be permanent, i.e., true for ever.
- **Estar**, on the other hand, expresses the opinion of the speaker which may or may not be shared by others. **Estar** expreses a fluctuating reality. Look at the following pairs.

- *Michael Jordad es alto.* Michael Jordan is tall.
  Mickey Rooney está alto en la foto. Mickey Rooney looks tall in the picture.
- *Bill Gates es rico.* Bill Gates is rich.
  Cindy Crawford está fea en la foto. Cindy Crawford looks ugly in the picture.
- *Don Knotts es nervioso.* Don Knotts is nervous (is a nervous person).
  Las alumnas están nerviosas porque tienen un examen final.
  The students are nervous because they have a final exam.

> **NOTE:** *Some adjectives express different meanings, depending whether they are used with **ser** or **estar**.*

- *El profesor es aburrido.* The teacher is boring.
  El profesor está aburrido. The teacher is bored.
- *La profesora es lista.* The teacher is clever.
  La profesora está lista. The teacher is ready.

- *El Papa es bueno.* The Pope is good (character, quality).

   El taco está bueno. The taco tastes good.
- *Saddam Hussein es malo.* Saddam Hussein is bad (evil).

   Julia Roberts está mala en la foto. Julia Roberts looks bad in
   the picture.

A. Read each sentence and decide whether you need to use **ser** or **estar**. Then, fill in the correct form of the verb (You may want to review chapters 5 and 6 before doing the following exercises).

1. ¿Cómo _____ Ud. hoy?

2. Mis zapatos _____ negros.

3. _____ las cuatro de la tarde.

4. Las tiendas no _____ abiertas ahora.

5. Su papá _____ del Perú, pero ahora _____ en California.

6. Nuestro hijo no _____ de acuerdo con nosotros.

7. Cuando recibo una "D" en un examen _____ furioso con mi
   profesor.

8. Lucia _____ bonita, inteligente y simpática.

9. ¡Qué elegante _____ (tú) esta* noche!

10. _____ un profesor aburrido y todos los estudiantes _____
   aburridos en su clase.

11. Los calcetines _____ limpios.

12. Esos regalos _____ para tu prima.

13. Su abuelo tiene sesenta años. No _____ muy viejo.

14. Las botas _____ muy baratas.

15. ¿_____ claro?

16. Las plumas _____ de plástico.

17. Maricarmen _____ doctora.

18. _____ necesario comer todos los días.

19. Cuando trabajamos mucho, _____ muy cansados.

20. Mi mamá _____ trabajadora, pero no _____ en la
   oficina hoy.

21. Siempre recibe "A" en sus exámenes. _____ una chica muy lista.

22. Casi siempre llega tarde a clase. Generalmente no _____ listo en
   la mañana.

---

* Notice how the accent mark helps distinguish one word from another: *esta*- this (fem.) as adjective; *está*- is; *ésta*- this one.

23. Pedro tiene veinte años. _____ muy joven.

24. _____ un hombre calmado, pero a veces _____ furioso.

25. La comida italiana _____ buena, pero esos espaguetis _____
    horribles.

26. Oscar Arias _____ el ex presidente de Costa Rica. _____ alto y
    moreno. Ahora _____ en Francia.

27. La biblioteca _____ en la calle Main, pero ahora _____
    cerrada.

28. ¿Cómo _____ tu nuevo novio? _____ cómico y pobre.

29. ¿A qué hora _____ su clase de matemáticas?

30. Quiero _____ doctora, pero no quiero _____ en la
    universidad ocho o nueve años.

B. Review. Fill in the appropriate form of *ser* or *estar*.

1. ¿Quién _____ el presidente?

2. ¿Cómo _____ Ud.? —Bien, gracias.

3. Santa Bárbara _____ en California.

4. Yo no _____ de acuerdo con Saddam Hussein.

5. Su camisa _____ blanca.

6. El laboratorio _____ cerrado ahora.

7. La blusa _____ de seda (*silk*).

8. ¿_____ Uds. cansados en la noche?

9. El bebé _____ muy joven.

10. ¿Comprendes? ¿ _____ claro?

C. Review. Translate.

1. The taco tastes very good.

_____

2. Where are you (*fam.*) at three a.m.?

_____

3. Guanajuato is located in Mexico.

_____

4. My father is not happy when I drive (*manejo*) fast.

_____

5. José Carreras is from Spain.

_____

6. This beer is for Francisco because he watches a lot of football games (*fútbol norteamericano*).

_____

7. Students are very poor, but they are glad to be in school.

_____

8. The French teacher (*masc.*) is very boring.

_____

9. How handsome you look today!

_____

10. We are Germans.

_____

11. She does not agree with you (*form.*).

_____

12. Are you (*fam.*) ready?

_____

13. The chair is made of metal.

_____

14. My grandparents are ready to go out.

_____

15. I want to be a math professor.

_____

16. Is it necessary to go to class on Fridays?

_____

17. His shirt is green.

_____

18. Is it clear?

_____

19. It's nine a.m.

_____

20. Are you (*pl.*) busy tonight?

_____

18 COMPARISONS

Comparisons of Inequality

To make comparisons of inequality (*comparaciones de desigualdad*) use
más (more),* **menos** (less) and **que** (than):

- Bill Gates es **más** rico **que** la profesora.

  Bill Gates is richer than the professor.
- La profesora es **menos** rica **que** Bill Gates.

  The professor is less rich than Bill Gates.
- Los coches pequeños son **más** económicos **que** los grandes.

  Small cars are more economical than big ones.
- Pancho tiene **más** clases **que** yo.

  Pancho has more classes than I.
- La profesora come **menos que** los estudiantes.

  The professor eats less than the students.
- Yo escribo **menos** rápido **que** mi hermano.

  I write less rapidly than my brother.

As you can see from the previous examples, the combination **más/menos**
que works with adjectives, nouns, and adverbs.

A. Add **más** or **menos** as appropriate.

1. Mi papá ($4 000) tiene _____ dinero que yo ($5).
2. La doctora (45 horas) trabaja _____ horas que la profesora
   (50 horas).
3. El dentista habla _____ que el paciente.
4. La mamá duerme _____ que el bebé.
5. Los exámenes de inglés son _____ difíciles que los de
   educación física.
6. Michael Jordan es _____ alto que Micky Rooney.
7. Roseanne es _____ cómica que nuestro profesor de
   matemáticas.
8. Mi hermano (200 libras) es _____ gordo que mi tía (135).

---

* In English **más** translates with the suffix "-er" when the adjective has no more than two syllables.

Irregular Comparatives

ADJECTIVES			ADVERBS		
bueno-a	**mejor**	*better*	bien	**mejor**	*better*
buenos-as	**mejores**	*better*	mal	**peor**	*worse*
malo-a	**peor**	*worse*			
malos-as	**peores**	*worse*			
viejo-a	**mayor**	*older*			
viejos-as	**mayores**	*older*			
joven	**menor**	*younger*			
jóvenes	**menores**	*younger*			

Remember that adjectives modify nouns and they have to agree with the nouns.

- "B" es una nota buena, pero "A" es mejor.
  "B" is a good grade, but "A" is better.
- Estos coch**es** son mejor**es** que aquellos.
  These cars are better than those.

Adverbs describe verbs and only have one form.
- Luis canta bien, pero nosotros cantamos mejor.
  Luis sings well, but we sing better.

B. Fill in the appropriate comparative from the right column.

1. Nuestro abuelo es _____ que nuestro papá.
2. Mi esposa cocina bien, pero yo cocino _____.
3. Su hermano es casado y vive en California.
   Su hermana _____ está en la escuela secundaria.
4. Estos libros son malos, pero esos son aun (*even*)
   _____.
5. Los Porsches son _____ que los Pintos.
6. Tú hablas francés _____ que Jacqueline.

menor
peores
mejores
peor
mayor
mejor

Comparisons of Equality
(*comparaciones de igualdad*)

Nouns
For nouns, use **tanto/tanta/tantos/tantas+noun+ como**:

- Luis bebe **tanta** cerveza **como** Pedro.

  Luis drinks as much beer as Pedro.

- Luis bebe **tanto** café **como** Pedro.

  Luis drinks as much coffee as Pedro.

- Los chicos compran **tantas** camisas **como** Uds.
  Boys buy as many shirts as you do.

- Las chicas compran **tantos** zapatos **como** nosotros.
  Girls buy as many shoes as we do.

C. Fill in the appropriate form of **tanto, tanta, tantos, tantas**.

1. Ellos compran _____ fruta como nosotros
2. Yo tengo _____ hermanos como tú.
3. Su papá no usa _____ zapatos como su mamá.
4. Los alumnos necesitan _____ dinero como las alumnas.
5. La profesora de francés enseña _____ clases como la
   profesora de alemán.
6. Nuestro tío come _____ tacos como yo.

Adjectives
To make comparisons of equality with adjectives, use **tan+ adjective+ como**:

- Luis es **tan** rico **como** Pedro.

  Luis is as rich as Pedro.

- Los chicos son **tan** inteligentes **como** las chicas.
  Boys are as intelligent as girls.

Adverbs
For adverbs, use **tan+ adverb+ como**:

- Luis habla español **tan** bien **como** Pedro.

  Luis speaks Spanish as well as Pedro.

- Los chicos escriben **tan** rápidamente **como** las chicas.
  Boys write as rapidly as girls.

Verbs

For verbs, use **tanto+como**:

- Luis duerme **tanto como** Pedro.

  Luis sleeps as much as Pedro.

- Nosotros trabajamos **tanto como** Uds.

  We work as much as you.

D. Fill in the appropriate form of **tan** or **tanto.**

1. Mi casa es _____ vieja como tu casa.

2. Ella estudia _____ como Ud.

3. Nuestros hermanos son _____ listos como Uds.

4. La doctora habla _____ rápido como el arquitecto.

5. El presidente no trabaja _____ como su esposa.

6. Yo no bebo _____ como mi profesor de inglés.

E. Fill in the appropriate form of **tan, tanto, tanta, tantos, tantas.**

1. Mi profesor de francés lee _____ libros como yo.

2. Nosotros somos _____ pobres como Uds.

3. El doctor escribe _____ bien como el dentista.

4. El hermano de Isabel compra _____ camisas como tú.

5. Uds. tienen _____ amigas como nosotras.

6. El bebé no duerme _____ como la mamá.

7. La señora López es _____ rica como la señora Smith.

8. Los alumnos tienen _____ exámenes como las alumnas.

9. Yo hablo _____ rápido como mi tío.

10. Los profesores trabajan _____ como los estudiantes.

F. Review. Fill in the appropriate comparative (**más, menos, que, tan, tanto, tanta, tantos, tantas, como, mayor, menor, peor, mejor**).

1. Nuestros primos bailan _____ bien como nosotros.

2. Los italianos beben _____ vino como los franceses.

3. Bill Gates no es _____ rico que yo.

4. Los abuelos de Mercedes son _____ que los padres de ella.

5. En general los hombres son _____ altos que las mujeres.

6. Francisco no canta _____ bien como Plácido Domingo.

7. Compramos (15) _____ sombreros que tú (10).

8. Mi papá (50 años) es _____ que mi mamá (54).

9. Los dentistas trabajan _____ horas como los doctores.

10. Él no come _____ como yo.

G. Review. Translate.

1. She speaks as slowly as I do.

_____

2. We don't drink less coffee than the French instructor (*m.*).

_____

3. Small cars are cheaper than big ones.

_____

4. Do plumbers earn (*ganar*) as much as doctors?

_____

5. I don't write as fast as my brother.

_____

6. Math exams are more difficult than Spanish exams.

_____

7. Are you (*fam.*) younger or older than your sister?

_____

8. Classes at 7:00 a.m. are worse than classes at 9:00 a.m.

_____

9. We eat as many enchiladas as you do (*pl.*).

_____

10. They don't have fewer friends than I.

_____

Comparisons

11. I buy as many shoes as you (*fam.*) do.

_____

12. We are as rich as our sisters.

_____

19 SABER and CONOCER

saber-to know	conocer-to know
yo **sé**	yo **conozco**
tú **sabes**	tú **conoces**
Ud. **sabe**	Ud. **conoce**
él, ella **sabe**	él, ella **conoce**
nosotros **sabemos**	nosotros **conocemos**
Uds. **saben**	Uds. **conocen**
ellos, ellas **saben**	ellos, ellas **conocen**

Saber and **Conocer** mean *to know* in English. However, each verb is used in different situations.

- **Conocer** means to be acquainted in general terms with something (a city, a country, etc.) or someone.

  Conozco a * *Pedro.* I know Pedro. (I am acquainted with Pedro).
  Conocemos Santa Bárbara. We know Santa Bárbara.

- **Conocer** can also mean *to meet* someone for the first time.

  Vamos a conocer a Gustavo esta noche. We are going to meet Gustavo tonight.

- **Saber,** on the other hand, means to have specific knowledge about something or someone.

  No sé el número de teléfono de Pedro. I don't know Pedro's phone number (i.e., a detail).

- **Saber** also means *to know how to* do something.

  Ella sabe cantar. She knows how ** to sing.

---

* When conocer is followed by a specific person, the preposition "a" is used after **conocer**.

** The word **how** in this construction is not translated in Spanish.

> **TIPS:** *1) make sure you know the conjugation for **saber** and for **conocer**.*
>
> *2) **conocer** must be followed by a noun (if the noun is a person, it will be preceded by the preposition **a**).*
>
> *3) **saber** can be followed by a noun, an infinitive, or an entire clause preceded by **que**.*

A. Read each sentence carefully and decide whether you need to use **saber** (S) or **conocer** (C).

1. Sabemos/Conocemos hablar francés.
2. Conocen/Saben a muchos estudiantes inteligentes.
3. La profesora sabe/conoce escribir poemas románticos.
4. En la fiesta vas a saber/conocer a mi hermano Francisco.
5. Plácido Domingo sabe/conoce cantar muy bien.
6. ¿Quieres conocer/saber el número de teléfono de la chica morena?
7. No conocemos/sabemos el nuevo restaurante chino.
8. Conozco/sé preparar enchiladas.
9. ¿Sabes/conoces jugar al béisbol?
10. Saben/conocen que este ejercicio es fácil.

B. Review. Fill in the correct form of **saber** or **conocer**.

1. Luis es muy popular. _____ a todos los estudiantes. Él no _____ bailar muy bien, pero todas las chicas quieren bailar con él.
2. Werner _____ contestar en muchas lenguas, pero no _____ cantar en italiano.
3. En una clase pequeña nosotros _____ a todos los alumnos, pero no _____sus números de seguro social.
4. Los bebés no _____ hablar muy bien.
5. Nosotros _____ que el profesor es bajo, gordo y simpático.
6. Yo _____ el lago, pero no _____ nadar.
7. Nosotros _____ que Santa María es una ciudad bonita.

8. ¿Uds. no _____ Harmony? Es una pequeña ciudad en
   la costa central de California.

C. Review. Translate.

1. I know Luis very well, but I don't know where he lives.

   _____

2. She wants to meet my Mexican friends.

   _____

3. We know how to make excellent enchiladas.

   _____

4. Do you (*formal*) know a lot of restaurants in California?

   _____

5. They know France, but they don't know how to speak French.

   _____

6. Pancho knows Mercedes, but does not know where she studies Italian.

   _____

7. The secretary knows how to type (*escribir a máquina*) rapidly.

   _____

8. The students know their teacher, but they do not know her telephone
   number.

   _____

9. Some doctors do not know their patients (*pacientes*) very well.

   _____

10. We know that the president is in Washington now.

   _____

Saber and Conocer

20 DIRECT OBJECT PRONOUNS

Pronouns (lit. "in the place of the nouns") are small words we use to replace nouns we have already mentioned. The idea is to avoid sounding too repetitive. Look at the following sentences:

I eat enchiladas. I eat enchiladas once a week. I like to eat enchiladas.
The second and third mention of "enchiladas" can be replaced with the direct object pronoun "them" and make the sentences less repetitive.

Direct Object Pronouns: Definition

The direct object noun or noun phrase answer the question *what* or *whom.*

    1. I eat *enchiladas. What* do you eat?
    2. I see the *teacher. Whom* do you see?
    3. I see *the elegant man wearing a white hat, yellow shirt, green pants, and purple shoes. Whom* do you see?

It is possible to replace "*enchiladas*" with the pronoun "*them*"; "*teacher*" with "*him*" or "*her*"; and "*the elegant man wearing a white hat, yellow shirt, green pants, and purple shoes*" with "*him.*"

A. Replace the direct objects with pronouns (it, them, him, her, them, me, you, us).

1. You speak <u>German</u>.

_____

2. We buy French <u>perfumes</u>.

_____

3. Your instructor gives <u>easy exams</u>.

_____

4. Louis calls <u>the competent doctors who speak Portuguese</u>.

_____

5. She takes <u>her brother</u> to school.

_____

6. I don't bother <u>my classmates</u>.

_____

Direct Object Pronouns In Spanish

me-me
te-you (*fam.*)*
nos-us
lo-it,him,you (*form.*)
la-it,her,you (*form.fem*)
los-them (objects and people), you (*pl.*)
las- them (objects and people), you (*pl. fem.*)

Position of Pronouns

Direct object pronouns (*los pronombres del complemento directo*) are placed **before** the verb:

- *Yo como las enchiladas.*

    *Yo **las** como.*
- *Uds. compran los carros.*

    *Uds. **los** compran.*
- *Nosotros **te** llamamos.*
- *Ellos **nos** miran.*

TIPS: *1) **Make sure** you know the meaning of the pronouns very well!*
*2) **te,lo,la,** mean "you" as the **object**; remember that if you is the **subject**, in Spanish it's translated as **tú, Ud., or Uds.***
*3) **nos** does <u>not</u> mean **we**; **nos** means **us**.*

B. Replace the direct object nouns with the corresponding pronouns.
    examples: Nosotros estudiamos <u>la lección</u>.
                     Nosotros <u>la</u> estudiamos.
           Uds. cantan <u>las canciones</u>.
                Uds. <u>las</u> cantan.

1. Ellos compran <u>la cerveza</u>.

_____

2. Pedro lee <u>los libros</u>.

_____

---

* The plural for "te" in Spain is "os." Since in Latin America "os" is not used, it will not be practiced in these exercises.

3. Tú necesitas <u>el dinero</u>.

_____

4. Nosotros conocemos <u>a las alumnas extranjeras.</u>

_____

5. Los alumnos quieren <u>las notas altas</u>.

_____

6. Uds. esperan <u>a los amigos</u>.

_____

7. Ellas invitan <u>a sus primos</u>.

_____

8. Los doctores llaman <u>al paciente</u>.

_____

C. Circle the appropriate pronoun. The underlined words serve as a clue.
1. <u>El coche</u> es barato. ¿Por qué no lo/la compramos?
2. <u>Las enchiladas</u> están ricas. ¿Los/Las comemos?
3. <u>Luisa</u> es muy simpática. Yo lo/la invito a mi fiesta.
4. Aquí está <u>nuestro</u> número de teléfono. ¿Los/Nos llaman Uds. más tarde?
5. <u>Tú</u> eres mi buen amigo. Yo te/las espero todas las mañanas.
6. <u>Ellos</u> son extranjeros. Nosotros no nos/los conocemos.

D. Fill in the appropriate pronoun. The underlined words serve as a clue.
1. Los chicos compran <u>el vino</u>, pero María no _____ bebe.
2. <u>Yo</u> soy muy cómico. Por eso mis amigos _____ invitan a muchas fiestas.
3. <u>Sr. Smith</u>, tenemos su número de teléfono. Nosotros _____ llamamos el sábado.
4. <u>Mercedes</u> es muy popular. Todos los alumnos _____ conocen.
5. Uds. comen <u>enchiladas</u> en casa, pero yo _____ como en mi restaurante favorito.
6. <u>Nosotros</u> trabajamos juntos y por eso ellos _____ esperan todos los días.

Answering Questions Using Direct Object Pronouns

1)In exercise "B, C, and D" verbs did not change. In the next exercises you will be doing something which is more typical in a conversation—answer questions using pronouns. Now the verb will change to agree with the subject of the answer.

> **examples**: *¿Ud. compra <u>los tacos</u>? Sí, (yo) los compro.*
>
> *¿Conoce Ud. <u>a mis primos</u>? Sí, (yo) los conozco.*
>
> *¿Miras (tú) <u>el programa interesante en español</u>?*
>
> *Sí, (yo) lo miro.*

2)As you have already learned, it is not necessary to use subject pronouns in Spanish since the verb endings already express them. However, you may wish to do so since it will help remind you to use the correct verb ending.

3) Negation: In negative sentences the word "no" is placed before the direct object pronouns:

> *Nosotros **no** lo conocemos.*
>
> *Ellos **no** las miran.*
>
> *Tú **no** me llamas.*

E. Answer the questions using direct object pronouns (*lo*-it, him; *la* -it, her; *los* -them, *las*-them).

1. ¿Ud. invita <u>a la profesora</u>?

_____

2. ¿Llama Ud. <u>a los señores</u>?

_____

3. ¿Tú conoces <u>a mis hermanos</u>?

_____

4. ¿Compra Ud. <u>las enchiladas que yo recomiendo</u>?

_____

5. ¿Sabes tú <u>todas las respuestas</u>?

_____

6. ¿Ud. trae <u>mucho vino</u> a la clase?

_____

7. ¿Esperas <u>a nuestros amigos</u>?

_____

8. ¿Ayuda Ud. <u>a los pobres</u>?

_____

F. Answer the questions using direct object pronouns (*lo*-you form. masc; *la*- you form. fem.).

    example: *¿Ud. me invita? Sí, yo lo (la) invito.*

1. ¿Ud. <u>me</u> llama? _____

2. ¿ <u>Me</u> conoce Ud.? _____

3. ¿Ud. <u>me</u> mira? _____

4. ¿<u>Me</u> busca Ud.? _____

5. ¿Ud. <u>me</u> espera? _____

G. Answer the questions using direct object pronoun (*te* -you fam.).

    example: *¿Tú me conoces? Sí, yo te conozco.*

1. ¿Tú <u>me</u> invitas? _____

2. ¿<u>Me</u> llamas tú? _____

3. ¿<u>Me</u> ves? _____

4. ¿Tú <u>me</u> esperas? _____

5. ¿<u>Me</u> buscas? _____

H. Answer the questions using direct object pronouns (*los, las* -you pl.).

    example: *¿Ud. nos llama? Sí, yo los (las) llamo.*

1. ¿Ud. <u>nos</u> busca? _____

2. ¿<u>Nos</u> mira Ud.? _____

3. ¿Ud. <u>nos</u> ve? _____

4. ¿Ud. <u>nos</u> espera? _____

5. ¿ <u>Nos</u> invita Ud.? _____

Position with Infinitives

Direct object pronouns may be attached to the infinitive of the verb or be placed in the usual position before the conjugated verb:

    Yo quiero comprar**las OR** Yo **las** quiero comprar.

    María desea llamar**nos OR** María **nos** desea llamar.

    Ellos van a invitar**te OR** Ellos **te** van a invitar.

I. Answer using direct object pronouns (*me, te, nos, lo, la, los, las*).
   example: *¿Ud. quiere beber el vino? Sí, yo quiero beberlo.* **AND**
   *Sí, yo **lo** quiero beber.*

1. ¿Ud. va a comer <u>las enchiladas</u>?

   _____

2. ¿Va Ud. a leer <u>los poemas</u>?

   _____

3. ¿Quiere Ud. invitar <u>a Luis</u>?

   _____

4. ¿Ud. desea llama<u>rme</u>?

   _____

5. ¿Necesita ver<u>nos</u> Ud.?

   _____

6. ¿Puede Ud. ayudar <u>a los estudiantes</u>?

   _____

J. Review. Answer the questions using direct object pronouns (**me, te, nos, lo, la, los, las**).

1. ¿Compra Ud. <u>las casas caras</u>? _____

2. ¿Miras <u>a los chicos guapos</u>? _____

3. ¿Estudian Uds. <u>los pronombres fáciles</u>?

   _____

4. ¿<u>Me</u> conoce Ud.? _____

5. ¿Los amigos <u>te</u> llaman por teléfono? _____

6. ¿Ves <u>a Pedro</u>? _____

7. ¿Los alumnos esperan <u>a los profesores</u>? _____

8. ¿Invitan Uds. <u>a las señoras bonitas y ricas</u>?

   _____

9. ¿Tú <u>me</u> buscas? _____

10. ¿Leen los chicos <u>los poemas románticos que explica la profesora</u>?

   _____

11. ¿Tocas <u>las canciones sentimentales que escuchas en la radio en español</u>?

   _____

12. ¿Nosotros <u>te</u> buscamos?

   _____

Direct Object Pronouns

13. ¿Deseas invitar <u>a los chicos</u>?

_____

14. ¿Pueden Uds. llamar<u>me</u> mañana?

_____

15. ¿Va Ud. a escribir <u>los poemas románticos</u>?

_____

K. Review. Translate.

1. I make the coffee and they drink it.

_____

2. She doesn't see us and we don't see her either.

_____

3. He is looking at them.

_____

4. Are you (*fam.*) calling me? Yes, I am calling you (*fam*).

_____

5. The teacher? The students wait for her everyday.

_____

6. Do you (*form.*) know Madonna? No, I don't know her, but I want to meet her.

_____

7. Is he going to invite us? Yes, he is going to invite all of you.

_____

8. Do you buy a lot of gifts? Yes, I buy them.

_____

9. The new song? Angelo can play it on the piano.

_____

10. The Mexican newspaper? Students read it in the library.

_____

Direct Object Pronouns

21 INDEFINITE and NEGATIVE WORDS

Indefinite Words

algo-something, anything
alguien-someone, anyone
alguno-some, any
alguna-some, any
algunos-some, any
algunas-some, any
siempre-always
también-also, too
(o)...o-(either)...or

- *Alguno* and *alguna* are adjectives. They precede and modify a noun that is not counted.
  *Necesito **alguna** manera de aprender los verbos.*
  I need some way to learn the verbs.
  *Queremos **algún*** concepto fácil.*
  We want some easy concept.

- *Algunos* and *algunas* are another way to say *unos* and *unas*. They are also adjectives and precede nouns that <u>can</u> be counted.
  *Quieren **algunas** cervezas alemanas.*
  They want some German beers.
  *Busco **algunos** diccionarios bilingües.*
  I am looking for some bilingual dictionaries.

A. Circle the appropriate indefinite word.

1. Todos los días estudian y *algún/siempre* sacan "A" en sus clases.
2. Buscamos tres o cuatro pantalones negros. También necesitamos *algunas/algunos* azules.

---

*When *alguno* is followed by a masculine noun, it becomes *algún*.

3. Voy a tomar el desayuno y *siempre/también* el almuerzo en un
   restaurante mexicano.
4. Miran *alguien/algunas* películas francesas.
5. *Alguien/algo* habla inglés y portugués.
6. Preparan *algún/algo* excepcional.

Negative Words
(*expresiones negativas*)

nada-nothing, not anything
nadie-no one, nobody, not anybody
ninguno-no, none, not any
ninguna-no, none, not any
nunca*-never
tampoco-neither, not either
(*ni*)...*ni*-(neither)...nor

- *Ninguno* and *ninguna* are adjectives and precede the nouns they modify.
  *No tengo **ningún**** coche italiano*. I don't have any Italian cars.
  *No compran **ninguna** cerveza francesa*. They don't buy any French
  beers.
- Note that *ningún* and *ninguna* are followed by a singular noun, but in
  English it's translated with the plural. (The forms *ningunos* and *ningunas*
  are not used).
- When a negative word is placed after a verb, Spanish uses a double and
  sometimes even a triple negative. This is grammatically correct in
  Spanish.
  *No compramos **nada** ahora*. We are not buying anything now.
  *No están **nunca** aquí el domingo*. ***Nunca** están aquí el domingo*.
      They are never here on Sunday.
  *No dan **nada** a **nadie***. They don't give anything to anyone.
  Nunca** compran **nada** a **nadie. They never buy anything to anyone.

---

*Jamás also means <u>never</u>, but is generally used in poetry or songs. It may be used after *nunca* —*nunca
jamás*— to mean "never again."
**When *ninguno* is followed by a masculine noun, it becomes *ningún*.

Indefinite and Negative Words

It's a good idea to learn the negative expressions in relation to their indefinite counterparts. Review the following chart before doing exercise "B."

algo-something, anything	*nada*-nothing, not anything, at all
alguien-someone, anyone	*nadie*-no one, nobody, not anybody
alguno-some, any	*ninguno*-no, none, not any
alguna-some, any	*ninguna*-no, none, not any
algunos-some, any	*ninguno*-no, none, not any
algunas-some, any	*ninguna*-no, none, not any
siempre-always	*nunca*-never
también-also, too	*tampoco*-neither, not either
(o)...o-(either)...or	*(ni)...ni*-(neither)...nor

B. Change from affirmative to negative.

1. Hay *algunos* restaurantes buenos en nuestra ciudad.

_____

2. *Alguien* habla ruso aquí.

_____

3. Estudiamos en casa *con frecuencia.*

_____

4. Tienen *algo* en la mano (*hand*).

_____

5. Yo *también* miro la tele los sábados.

_____

6. Quieren *algún* sistema para entender los verbos irregulares.

_____

7. Sirven enchiladas *o* tacos.

_____

8. *Alguien* prepara la cena ahora.

_____

9. Hay *algunos* libros en la mesa.

_____

Indefinite and Negative Words

10. *Siempre* habla francés en su clase de español.

_____

11. Uds. van a Europa. Nosotros *también*.

_____

12. ¿Le gusta *algo*?

_____

C. Review. Translate.

1. We don't drink anything in class.

_____

2. I never prepare my homework on my motorcycle.

_____

3. Luis has something in his pocket (*bolsillo*).

_____

4. We are not going to Portugal either.

_____

5. She doesn't want coffee or tea.

_____

6. Someone is reading now.

_____

7. No one in my family speaks German.

_____

8. There are some excellent hotels in our city.

_____

9. Are there any French restaurants in Santa Barbara?

_____

10. There aren't any easy classes.

_____

11. I need some way of finishing this exercise quickly.

_____

12. They are not buying anything.

_____

22 FORMAL COMMANDS

Commands (*mandatos*) are used to ask or tell someone to do something. You have probably noticed some of the following commands your instructor used in class:

¡**Repita(n)**! Repeat! ¡**Esuche(n)**! Listen!

Commands for -**ar** verbs

Singular	Plural
¡Cante Ud.!	¡Canten Uds.!
¡Hable Ud.!	¡Hablen Uds.!

- As you can see, the ending is -**e** for the singular, and -**en** for the plural.

Commands for -**er** and -**ir** verbs

Singular	Plural
¡Coma Ud.!	¡Coman Uds.!
¡Escriba Ud.!	¡Escriban Uds.!

- As you can see, the ending is -**a** for the singular, and -**an** for the plural.
- Note that *Ud.* and *Uds.* may be used with Spanish commands. If you use them, they are placed **after** the verb.
- **Negative commands**: put the word "**no**" in front of the verb:

    ¡Coma Ud.! ¡**No** coma Ud.!
- **Familiar commands**: see Chapter 32.

A. Change the singular commands to plural ones. In this "easy" exercise you will simply add an "**n**" to the verb to make it plural. As you do the exercise, note the infinitive and review the meaning for yourself.

examples: ¡Coma Ud.! *¡Coman Uds.!* Eat!

¡Llame Ud. a los chicos! *¡Llamen Uds. a los chicos!* Call the boys!

1. ¡Trabaje Ud. mucho! _____

2. ¡Cene Ud. a las seis! _____

3. ¡Fume Ud. ahora ! _____

4. ¡Desayune Ud. en casa! _____

5. ¡Enseñe Ud. bien! _____

6. ¡Compre Ud. la casa nueva! _____

7. ¡Regrese Ud. temprano! _____

8. ¡Lea Ud. la novela! _____

9. ¡Beba Ud. la leche! _____

10. ¡Escriba Ud. la carta! _____

B. Change the singular commands to plural ones. Just like in exercise **A,** in this exercise you will simply ad an "**n**" to the verb to make it plural. As you do the exercise, notice the stem-changing verbs and the irregular ones. Again, review the infinitive and the meaning for yourself.

1. (empezar) ¡Empiece Ud. a estudiar! _____

2. (practicar) ¡Practique Ud. toda la lección! _____

3. (almorzar) ¡Almuerce Ud. con su esposo! _____

4. (pagar) ¡Pague Ud. la cuenta! _____

5. (jugar) ¡Juegue Ud. a la lotería! _____

6. (sacar) ¡Saque Ud. la foto! _____

7. (estar) ¡Esté Ud. listo para el examen! _____

8. (escribir) ¡Escriba Ud. la tarea en casa! _____

9. (volver) ¡Vuelva Ud. aquí mañana! _____

10. (dormir) ¡Duerma Ud. ocho horas! _____

11. (pedir) ¡Pida Ud. el dinero! _____

12. (repetir) ¡Repita Ud. la oración! _____

13. (decir) ¡Diga Ud. la verdad! _____

14. (poner) ¡Ponga Ud. el dinero en el banco! _____

15. (ser) ¡Sea Ud. buena! _____

16. (dar) ¡Dé Ud. dinero a los pobres! _____

17. (ir) ¡Vaya Ud. al laboratorio! _____

18. (saber) ¡Sepa Ud. los verbos irregulares! _____

19. (abrazar) ¡Abrace (*hug*) Ud. a su mamá! _____

20. (llegar) ¡Llegue Ud. a tiempo! _____

21. (traer) ¡Traiga Ud. su perro a la clase! _____

22. (salir) ¡Salga Ud. con la chica extranjera! _____

C. Give advice to your teacher. Use affirmative or negative commands.

example: Su profesor habla demasiado. *¡No hable Ud. demasiado!*

1. come demasiado _____

2. llega a clase tarde _____

3. no paga sus cuentas _____

4. fuma mucho _____

5. no bebe leche _____

6. no repite las explicaciones _____

7. duerme dieciséis horas _____

8. sólo pide ensalada para la cena _____

9. sale de casa a las cuatro de la mañana _____

10. va al bar todas la noches _____

11. no trae regalos a la clase _____

12. siempre da tarea _____

D. Give advice to Mr. and Mrs. Gómez. Use affirmative or negative commands as appropriate.

example: El señor y la señora Gómez comen mucho.

¡No coman Uds. mucho!

1. ponen mucho azúcar en el café _____

2. nunca salen de casa _____

3. nunca regresan a México _____

4. cenan a las once de la noche _____

5. nunca juegan con su perro _____

6. nunca dicen la verdad _____

7. siempre almuerzan en McDonald's _____

8. nunca abrazan (*hug*) a su hijo _____

9. nunca sacan fotos de sus nietos _____

10. no saben nuestros problemas _____

11. duermen cuatro horas _____

12. siempre llegan tarde _____

COMMANDS WITH OBJECT AND REFLEXIVE PRONOUNS

- With **negative** commands, the pronouns are placed in front of the verb.

  *No coma el taco. No **lo** coma.*

  *No **le** hablen a Pancho. No **le** hablen.*

  *No **se** siente aquí. No **se** báñen ahora.*

- With **affirmative** commands, the pronouns are attached to the verb and a written accent will also be necessary.

  *Compre Ud. los regalos. Cómpre**los**.*

  *Diga Ud. la verdad. Díga**la**.*

  *Tráiga**nos** el vino. Lláme**nos**.*

  Siéntese. Lávense.

- The accent mark will be placed on the stressed syllable of the verb form (the syllable where the voice goes up).

E. Change from affirmative to negative. Note the position of the pronouns and that of the written accent mark.

> **examples**: Dígala. *No la diga.*
>
> Cómprenlos. *No los compren.*
>
> Siéntese. *No se siente.*

1. Fúmela. _____

2. Quítense. _____

3. Escríbanla. _____

4. Ábralos._____

5. Póngase. _____

6. Créame._____

7. Léalos._____

8. Practíquenlas. _____

9. Tómelas. _____

10. Enséñelo. _____

11. Búsquenos. _____

12. Báñese. _____

13. Sírvala._____

14. Acuéstese. _____

15. Repítala._____

16. Déme. _____

17. Óiganos._____

18. Vístase. _____

19. Háganlos._____

20. Piénselo. _____

21. Levántense. _____

22. Empiécela._____

23. Póngalo._____

24. Escríbale._____

25. Ciérrelo._____

F. Write the accent mark on the appropriate vowel.

1. Haganlos	2. Saquela	3. Digale	4. Sirvala
5. Bebalo	6. Arreglelo	7. Vealo	8. Comala
9. Llamenos	10. Busquelo	11. Cantenla	12. Hablele
13. Levantese	14. Bañense	15. Diviertase	16. Acuestense

G. Review. Write the formal comands.

	Ud.	Uds.
1. estudiar		
2. escribir		
3. empezar		
4. volver		
5. hacer		
6. ponerse		
7. ir		
8. venir		
9. despertarse		
10. traer		
11. quitarse		
12. decir		
13. vestirse		
14. levantarse		
15. pedir		

H. Review. Translate.

1. Buy the car. Buy it now.

_____

2. Go to school. Go every day.

_____

3. Enjoy yourselves.

_____

4. Don't go out (*pl.*) tonight.

_____

5. Come here on Friday (*pl*).

_____

6. Get up.

_____

7. Don't sell (*pl.*) your house. Don't sell it now.

_____

8. Don't look for us now, look for us tomorrow.

_____

9. Don't take off your jacket.

_____

10. Start your lessons. Start them now.

_____

11. Students, put the pens on the table. Don't put them in your coffee.

_____

12. Put on (*pl.*) your sweaters.

_____

13. Sleep seven hours, but don't sleep in class.

_____

Formal Commands

14. Sell your motorcycle. Sell it today.

_____

15. Order the steak and eat it.

_____

16. Wake up (*pl.*).

_____

17. Don't bring us your problems.

_____

18. Take two aspirins and <u>don't</u> call me in the morning.

_____

19. Don't take a bath now.

_____

20. Think about it.

_____

TIP: *When you use the command forms, it's always a good idea to complete them with "por favor." It may be that your tone of voice sounds "bossy". "Por favor" insures politeness.*

23 INDIRECT OBJECT PRONOUNS AND PRESENT OF *DAR* AND *DECIR*

Indirect object nouns and pronouns are in some ways similar to the direct object nouns and pronouns. This section will deal mostly with indirect objects. For a contrast between direct and indirect object pronouns, see Chapter 24 which contrasts these two grammar points.

Indirect Object Pronouns: Definition

The indirect object noun or noun phrase answers the question *to whom* or *for whom* * something is done, although the word "to"** is often not expressed in English.

1. *To whom* do you speak?

   (Or, in less formal English: *Who* do you speak *to*?)

   I speak <u>to the teacher</u>.

2. *To whom* do you write letters?

   (Or, *Who* do you write letters *to*?)

   We write letters <u>to our friends.</u>

3. *To whom* do they send money?

   (Or, *Who* do they send money *to*?

   They send <u>us</u> money.

4. *For whom* does he open the door?

   (Or, *Who* does he open the door *for*?)

   He opens the door <u>for the boys</u>.

---

* Remember that direct objects answer the question *what* or *whom* and can refer to objects as well as people.

** With a few verbs such as "comprar" or "vender" the preposition can be "to" , "for", or "from". The English meaning can vary, depending on the context:

    Ella me compra helado can mean <u>She buys ice cream from me</u> OR <u>She buys me ice cream.</u>

    Pedro nos vende el libro can mean <u>Pedro sells us (to us) the book</u> OR <u>Pedro sells the book for us.</u>

A. Underline the words expressing the indirect object. If you have trouble, think of a question starting with *to whom* or *for whom* that the sentence could answer.

example: Our family donated a million dollars to the Santa Maria Valley Children's Museum.

(**think**): *To whom* did your family donate a million dollars?

(**answer**): the Santa Maria Valley Children's Museum

1. The college gives scholarships to the poor students.
2. I am going to buy my husband a new cookbook.
3. He is doing the secretary a big favor.
4. She opened the door for the man with the baby carriage.
5. I teach students easy and difficult grammar points.
6. You recommended a good restaurant to me.
7. The doctor sent us a huge bill.
8. He loaned her twenty dollars.
9. We sold them our Italian car.
10. She wrote you a long letter.

Indirect Object Pronouns In Spanish

me-to me, for me
te-to you, for you (*fam.*)
nos-to us, for us
le- to or for him, her, you (*form.*)
les-to or for them, you (*pl.*)

TIP: *me, te, and nos, are exactly the same forms as the direct object pronouns. These three cause no problems at all. The only difference is that me means to me in English instead of simply me, etc. In essence, whether in English you have me, to me, or for me,* the Spanish word is always me.*

---

* "For me" preceded by the verb "ser" is not an indirect object pronoun, but rather a prepositional one. It translates in Spanish "para mí."

Indirect Object Pronouns and Present of Dar and Decir

Examples In Spanish With Indirect Object Pronouns

1. *Yo te hablo*. I speak to you.
2. *Ellos me escriben cartas*. They write me letters.
3. *Luisa nos manda flores*. Luisa sends us flowers.
4. *Nosotros le damos dinero*. We give him (her, you) money.**
5. *Yo les digo mentiras*. I tell them (or you pl.) lies.

B. Fill in the indirect object pronouns (*los pronombres del complemento indirecto*).

1. Ud. _____ escribe cartas (a mí).
2. Ellos no _____ venden el coche (a nosotros).
3. La profesora _____ explica la gramática (a ti).
4. Nosotros _____ compramos regalos (a Ud.).
5. Tú _____ dices la verdad (a ellos).
6. Luisa _____ da el dinero (a Pedro y a mí).
7. Él no _____ presta su bolígrafo (a ti).
8. Yo no _____ mando flores (a Uds.).
9. Uds. _____ abren la puerta (a mí).
10. Bill Clinton _____ hace el favor (a nosotros).

Required Redundancy

In English, we use *either* an indirect object noun *or* an equivalent indirect object pronoun:

either: I speak to Pedro.

or: I speak to him.

In Spanish, however, when an indirect object noun appears in a sentence, the counterpart indirect object pronoun will almost always be expressed as well.

example: *Yo le hablo a Pedro.*

I speak to Pedro. (Lit. I to him speak to Pedro).

Notice that in the example there is both an indirect object pronoun (le) and an indirect object noun (a Pedro). To English speakers this sounds illogical. Why do you need both? The answer is simply that Spanish requires it.

** In example # 4 one may add *a él, a ella,* or *a Ud.* to clarify the meaning of *le*. The same principle applies to # 5 where one may add *a ellos, a ellas,* or *a Uds*. In general, the context is enough to avoid ambiguity. Remember that *le* or *les* are however mandatory.

Indirect Object Pronouns and Present of Dar and Decir

Languages are often not logical and their grammar is based on tradition or culture rather than rational arguments.

> *Ud. les escribe a los chicos.* You write to the boys.
>
> *Nosotros le cantamos canciones a Luisa.* We sing songs to Luisa.
>
> *Tú les mandas flores a tus padres.* You send flowers to your parents.

In Spanish, whenever you use an indirect object noun, you must also include the indirect object pronoun in the same sentence.

C. Fill in the appropriate indirect object pronouns (notice the required redundancy).

1. Uds. _____ mandan chocolates *a sus amigos.*
2. Yo _____ digo buenos días *a mi esposo.*
3. Tú _____ escribes poemas cómicos *a tu novio.*
4. Nosotros _____ hacemos favores *a la doctora.*
5. Ellas _____ venden su computadora *a los estudiantes.*
6. Los chicos _____ explican el problema *a mi abuelo.*

D. Fill in the appropriate indirect object pronouns (the underlined word will serve as a clue to which pronoun you should add).

1. En clase <u>nosotros</u> tenemos que contestar porque la profesora _____ hace preguntas.
2. Yo _____ hablo por teléfono porque <u>tú</u> no me escribes.
3. Ellos _____ dicen sus secretos porque <u>yo</u> soy su buen amigo.
4. <u>Tus amigos</u> son pobres. Por eso tú no _____ pides dinero.
5. Cuando <u>Ud.</u> entra en un restaurante pequeño, el camarero _____ trae el menú y _____ indica una mesa desocupada.
6. Cuando mi esposa y yo regresamos a casa, <u>nuestros</u> hijos _____ explican sus problemas.
7. Cuando <u>yo</u> estoy enfermo, mi hija _____ prepara sopa de pollo (chicken soup).
8. <u>Sus amigos</u> están a dieta. Por eso Ud. _____ ofrece ensaladas.
9. Nosotros tenemos alergias a las flores. Entonces <u>nuestros</u> amigos _____ mandan chocolates para el Día de San Valentín.
10. Cuando <u>tú</u> vienes a mi casa, yo _____ sirvo mi plato favorito.

E. Answer the questions using the indirect object pronoun **"te"** (to you).

   example: *¿Tú me contestas? Sí, yo te contesto.*

1. ¿Tú <u>me</u> escribes?

_____

2. ¿<u>Me</u> hablas?

_____

3. ¿<u>Me</u> explicas la lección?

_____

4. ¿<u>Me</u> das el dinero?

_____

5. ¿<u>Me</u> mandas tarjetas?

_____

6. ¿<u>Me</u> dices la verdad?

_____

F. Answer the questions using the indirect object pronoun **"le"** (to you, formal).

   example: *¿Ud. me escribe en inglés? Sí, yo le escribo en inglés (a Ud.).*

1. ¿Ud. <u>me</u> manda chocolates?

_____

2. ¿Ud. <u>me</u> dice mentiras?

_____

3. ¿Ud. <u>me</u> presta el dinero?

_____

4. ¿<u>Me</u> contesta Ud. en español?

_____

5. ¿<u>Me</u> sirve Ud. la comida?

_____

6. ¿<u>Me</u> explica Ud. la lección?

G. Answer the questions using the indirect object pronouns **"le** or **les"** (to him, to her, to them).

   example: *¿Ud. les explica todo a sus amigos? Sí, yo les explico todo (a ellos).*

1. ¿Ud. <u>le</u> dice mentiras <u>a su novio</u>?

_____

Indirect Object Pronouns and Present of Dar and Decir

2. ¿ Ud. <u>le</u> habla <u>a Luis</u>?

_____

3. ¿Ud. <u>les</u> da dinero <u>a los pobres</u>?

_____

4. ¿Ud. <u>les</u> sirve el pastel <u>a los clientes</u>?

_____

5. ¿<u>Les</u> canta Ud. canciones románticas <u>a sus amigos</u>?

_____

H. Answer the questions using the indirect object pronoun **"les"** (to you pl.).
example: _¿Ud. nos canta en francés? Sí, yo les canto en francés (a Uds.)._

1. ¿Ud. <u>nos</u> pregunta en inglés?

_____

2. ¿<u>Nos</u> sirves las hamburguesas?

_____

3. ¿<u>Nos</u> dan el boleto Uds.?

_____

4. ¿<u>Nos</u> compran regalos Uds.?

_____

5. ¿<u>Nos</u> escriben Uds. cartas?

_____

I. Answer the questions using the indirect object pronoun **"me"** (to me).
example: _¿Los amigos te escriben? Sí, ellos me escriben._

1. ¿Los chicos <u>te</u> preguntan?

_____

2. ¿La alumna <u>te</u> sirve la sopa?

_____

3. ¿Los profesores <u>te</u> dicen la verdad?

_____
_____

4. ¿Luis <u>te</u> explica las respuestas?

_____

5. ¿Bill Clinton <u>te</u> trae el café?

_____

Indirect Object Pronouns and Present of Dar and Decir

J. Answer the questions using the indirect object pronouns **"te** or **le"** (to you).

> **example:** *¿Los turistas me pagan el viaje? Sí, ellos te pagan el viaje.* **OR** *Sí, ellos le pagan el viaje (a Ud.).*

1. ¿Los profesores <u>me</u> mandan flores?

_____

2. ¿Los amigos <u>me</u> hacen el favor?

_____

3. ¿Tus padres <u>me</u> compran regalos?

_____

4. ¿Los cantantes <u>me</u> cantan canciones románticas?

_____

5. ¿Los chicos <u>me</u> preparan la cena?

_____

K. Answer the questions using the indirect object pronouns **"nos** or **les"** (to us, to you pl.).

> **example:** *¿El profesor nos manda chocolates? Sí, él nos manda chocolates.* (if the person answering is part of the group).
> *Sí, él les manda chocolates (a Uds.).* (The person answering is not part of the group, i.e., gets no chocolates).

1. ¿María <u>nos</u> dice la verdad?

_____

2. ¿El doctor <u>nos</u> hace el favor?

_____

3. ¿El camarero <u>nos</u> trae el menú?

_____

4. ¿Luisa <u>nos</u> escribe la carta?

_____

5. ¿Los secretarios <u>nos</u> abren la puerta?

_____

L. Answer the questions using indirect object pronouns (two ways).

> **examples:** *¿Ud. me va a escribir? Sí, yo le voy a escribir (a Ud.).* **AND** *Sí, yo voy a escribirle (a Ud.).*

1. ¿Ud. <u>me</u> va a dar su número de teléfono?

_____

_____

Indirect Object Pronouns and Present of Dar and Decir

2. ¿Tú les deseas comprar regalos a los chicos?

_____

_____

3. ¿Ud. nos quiere explicar la lección?

_____

_____

4. ¿Uds. nos van a mandar chocolates?

_____

_____

5. ¿Ud. me puede prestar el coche?

_____

_____

Present Tense of

Dar (to give)	Decir (to say, tell)
yo doy	yo digo
tú das	tú dices
Ud. da	Ud. dice
él, ella da	él, ella dice
nosotros/nosotras damos	nosotros/nosotras decimos
Uds. dan	Uds. dicen
ellos, ellas dan	ellos, ellas dicen

The verbs **dar** and **decir** are normally used with an indirect object pronoun.
- Yo le doy regalos a mi papá.

  I give my dad gifts.
- Nosotros les decimos la verdad a nuestros amigos.

  We tell our friends the truth.

M. Fill in the blanks with the appropriate form of the present of *dar* or *decir* and an indirect pronoun.

   1. Yo les _____ (dar) dinero a los pobres, pero no _____ doy dinero todos los días.

   2. Tú le _____ (decir) "buenos días" a tu profesora en la mañana. En la tarde tú _____ dices "buenas tardes".

Indirect Object Pronouns and Present of Dar and Decir

3. Nosotros no te _____ (dar) muchos exámenes, pero
   _____ damos muchas pruebas.

4. Ellos nos _____ (decir) sus secretos, pero no _____
   dicen los secretos por teléfono.

5. Uds. no les _____ (dar) chocolates a sus amigos. Uds.
   _____ dan flores.

6. Luis me _____ (decir) cosas cómicas, pero no _____
   dice nada durante el examen final.

N. Review. Answer the questions using indirect object pronouns.

1. ¿Tú me escribes en francés?

   _____

2. ¿Me presta Ud. su coche?

   _____

3. ¿Les hablas a los doctores en portugués?

   _____

4. ¿Ud. nos canta canciones italianas?

   _____

5. ¿Los amigos te sirven la cerveza?

   _____

6. ¿La secretaria me manda flores?

   _____

7. ¿Julio Iglesias nos hace los favores?

   _____

8. ¿Quieres darme tu número de teléfono?

   _____

9. ¿Van Uds. a comprarnos regalos?

   _____

10. ¿Puede Ud. traerme el menú?

    _____

11. ¿Ud. le explica el problema a su papá?

    _____

12. ¿Uds. les dicen la verdad a sus novios?

    _____

O. Review. Translate.

1. The students? They speak to me in English, but I always answer them in Spanish.

_____

2. Donald Trump? I am sending him an expensive gift.

_____

3. The teacher (*masc.*) gives us easy exams.

_____

4. The doctor? Can he explain the problem to me?

_____

5. The secretary? We are going to tell her the truth.

_____

6. The psychologist (*fem.*) is not going to give you (*form.*) her telephone number.

_____

7. My father is buying us a very good dictionary.

_____

8. The customers? The waiter serves them breakfast.

_____

9. Mary? She is saving you (*pl.*) your seats.

_____

10. Your cousin Jack? I never lend him any money.

_____

11. Pedro and I can do the favor for your (*fam.*) uncle.

_____

12. Are you going to prepare dinner for all the students?

_____

13. My sister is opening the window for you (*form.*).

_____

14. The boys always ask me difficult questions.

_____

15. Don Juan? Carmen does not want to give him her phone number.

_____

24 DIRECT VS. INDIRECT OBJECT PRONOUNS

Similarities

Direct and **indirect object pronouns** (*los pronombres del complemento directo e indirecto*) in Spanish are alike in several ways:

1) They come before the conjugated verb or are attached to the end of the infinitive.

2) **Me**, **te**, **nos** are the same whether used as direct or indirect object pronouns. Their English meanings, however, are slightly different. As direct object pronouns **me**, **te**, and **nos** mean <u>me</u>, <u>you</u> (fam.), and <u>us</u>; as indirects they mean <u>to me</u>, <u>to you</u> (fam.), and <u>to us</u> (remember that instead of **"to"** the preposition can sometimes be **"for"** and in a few cases even **"from"**). In essence, whether you are translating **me** or **to me**, **you** or **to you**, **us** or **to us**, the Spanish equivalents are the same.

Differences

1) Remember that many verbs in Spanish take the personal **"a"** when they are followed by a person. In these cases **"a"** does **not** translate in English and the person preceded by **"a"** is the **direct** object. Some very common verbs that require the personal **"a"** are *llamar, invitar, buscar, mirar, ver, conocer, esperar, oír,* etc.

> **example:** *Yo veo a Luis.* I see Luis.
> *Ellos invitan a mi prima.* They invite my cousin.
> *María conoce a tu abuelo.* Maria knows your grandfather

2) Remember that verbs requiring an indirect object express some kind of exchange of information or goods—give, send, sell, tell, write, explain, ask, loan, answer, etc. The person who receives the action is the indirect object; the thing received is the direct.

A. Identify the direct and indirect objects by marking a "D" or "I" above the underlined words or phrases.

1. Every week, he gives <u>money</u> <u>to his church</u>.

2. We are going to buy <u>our son</u> <u>a new bike</u>.

3. She is preparing <u>an easy exam</u> <u>for you</u>.

4. I am doing <u>the doctor</u> <u>a big favor</u>.

5. They opened <u>the door</u> <u>for the children</u>.

6. The teacher explains <u>the difficult grammar points</u> <u>to the students.</u>

7. You suggest <u>good classes</u> <u>to me</u>.

8. Are you calling <u>the competent plumber who speaks Spanish</u>?

9. We speak <u>to our daughter</u> every day.

10. He invites <u>his classmates</u> to a party.

B. Identify the direct and indirect objects by marking a "D" or "I" above the underlined words or phrases.

1. Luis llama <u>a sus amigos.</u>

2. Uds. les escriben <u>cartas</u>.

3. Tú buscas <u>a los chicos que hablan francés.</u>

4. Ellos <u>nos</u> mandan <u>flores</u>.

5. Los niños <u>te</u> traen <u>regalos</u>.

6. Sus padres <u>les</u> hacen <u>favores</u>.

7. Nosotros <u>te</u> decimos <u>mentiritas</u>.

8. Los pacientes <u>le</u> explican <u>el problema</u> <u>al doctor.</u>

9. Yo <u>te</u> vendo <u>mi coche viejo</u>.

10. Ella <u>nos</u> va a prestar <u>su motocicleta</u>.

Direct Vs. Indirect Object Pronouns

C. Review. Translate.

1. She is doing him a favor.

_____

2. We are looking at you (*form.*), but we are also looking at her.

_____

3. He is buying them a very expensive gift.

_____

4. The tourists are inviting you (*pl.*), but they are not inviting her.

_____

5. They are waiting for him.

_____

6. He is calling her.

_____

7. The teacher is opening the window for them.

_____

8. My grandparents are sending you (*form.*) chocolates.

_____

9. I see them (*masc.*) in class.

_____

10. They are going to write her a long letter.

_____

11. We want to ask him his phone number.

_____

12. He is helping you (*pl. masc.*).

_____

13. Your (*form.*) friend is lending them his car.

_____

Direct Vs. Indirect Object Pronouns

14. I don't know her very well.

_____

15. She cannot tell you (*fam.*) everything.

_____

_____

16. Mr. Ortega is giving her his recipe (*receta*) for tamales.

_____

LO, LA, LOS, LAS/ LE, LES

D. Translate. (**Lo**-it, him, you form.), (**la**-it, her, you form. fem.), (**los**-them, you pl.) (**las**-them, you pl.).

1. Mary? I am not inviting her to the party.

_____

2. The boys? We don't know them very well.

_____

3. The enchiladas? They are preparing them right now.

_____

4. The long novels? Luis is reading them.

_____

5. The doctor? They are calling him soon.

_____

6. The new car? Frank is not buying it.

_____

7. Are you (*pl.*) inviting us? Yes, we are inviting you.

_____

8. Is Pedro looking at the girls? Yes, he is looking at them, but he can't see them very well.

_____

Direct Vs. Indirect Object Pronouns

9. Are you (*form.*) looking for your brother? Yes, I am looking for him.

_____

10. Is the teacher waiting for you (*pl.*)? No, he never waits for us; we are always waiting for him.

_____

_____

E. Translate. **Le** (to* him, to her, to you), **les** (to them, to you pl.)

1. We are closing the windows for you (*form.*).

_____

2. The president? We are writing him a long letter.

_____

3. The doctors? I am not sending them any money.

_____

4. Pedro's brother? Mary is buying him a gift.

_____

5. The students? The teacher is doing them a favor.

_____

6. The boys? The girls open the door for them.

_____

7. My grandparents? I am writing them nice letters.

_____

8. Luisa's dad? She is serving him enchiladas tonight.

_____

9. The customers? The waiter is bringing them their salads.

_____

_____

* Remember that sometimes the preposition is "for" instead of "to."

Direct Vs. Indirect Object Pronouns

10. The children? Their teacher is teaching them English.

_____

F. Review. Translate.

1. Francisco? I speak to him in class.

_____

2. The car? We need to look for it after class.

_____

3. The teachers? Linda is inviting them.

_____

4. The house? My parents are selling it.

_____

5. The customers? The waiters are serving them tamales.

_____

6. The letters? The students are sending them this afternoon.

_____

7. Jennifer and I are doing her dad a favor.

_____

8. The gifts? The secretary is bringing them later.

_____

9. They are opening the door for you.

_____

10. The poems? I don't want to write them.

_____

25 GUSTAR

• **Gustar** ("to like" or lit. "to be pleasing to") does not normally conjugate. It is used primarily in the third person as **gusta** if the subject is singular and **gustan** if it is plural.

1. Me gusta la clase. *I like the class (The class is pleasing to me).*
2. Nos gusta la clase. *We like the class (The class is pleasing to us).*
3. Me gustan las clases. *I like the classes (The classes are pleasing to me).*
4. Nos gustan las clases. *We like the classes (The classes are pleasing to us).*
5. ¿Te gusta esquiar? *Do you like to ski? (Is skiing pleasing to you?).*
6. Les gusta hablar. *They like to speak. (Speaking is pleasing to them).*

• In examples # 1 & 2 **gusta** is used because the subject **la clase** is singular. In examples # 3 & 4 **gustan** is used because the subject **las clases** is plural. In examples # 5 & 6 **gusta** is used because the infinitive is the subject (an infinitive is considered a singular subject).

• The subject comes at the end and determines whether you use **gusta** or **gustan**. At the beginning, you need to use the indirect object pronouns **me**, **te**, **le**, **nos**, or **les**.

A. Fill in **gusta** or **gustan**.

1. Me _____ el español.
2. Nos _____ la cafetería.
3. Le _____ los poemas románticos.
4. ¿No te _____ cocinar espaguetis?
5. Les _____ hablar portugués.
6. Me _____ las películas de horror.
7. ¿Te _____ las clases este semestre?
8. Nos _____ las canciones cubanas.

9. Me _____ los niños pequeños.

10. No les _____ los exámenes orales.

- If you use **gustar** with a name, you need to start with the preposition **a**:

  A Francisco le gustan las clases. *Francisco likes the classes (The classes are pleasing to Francisco).*

  A mis amigos les gusta la música. *My friends like music (Music is pleasing to my friends).*

B. Complete te sentences. You may need to fill in the preposition **a**, the appropriate indirect object pronoun (**me, te, le, les, nos**), and **gusta** or **gustan**.

1. _____ los doctores _____ gusta jugar al golf los miércoles.

2. _____ la profesora _____ gustan los bailes colombianos.

3. _____ mi papá _____ gusta cantar, pero no le _____ bailar.

4. ¿_____ tu novia le _____ ir al cine en la tarde?

5. _____ los niños no _____ gustan las verduras.

6. ¿ _____ los pacientes _____ _____ las inyecciones?

7. _____ mi mamá no _____ _____ la música moderna.

8. _____ sus hermanos _____ _____ dormir muchas horas.

- **Gustaría/gustarían** mean "would like."

C. Review. Translate.

1. I like Spanish, but I don't like exams.

_____

2. Do you (*fam.*) like to dance?

_____

3. Does your (*form.*) dad like wine?

_____

4. We don't like to cook, but we like to eat.

_____

5. Do you (*form.*) like big classes?

_____

6. Mary likes French songs, but she doesn't like to sing.

_____

7. We like Japanese cars.

_____

8. Do your (*fam.*) brothers like horror movies?

_____

9. I would like to go to Madrid.

_____

10. Do you (*pl.*) like the beach?

_____

11. Does your (*form.*) math instructor (*fem.*) like beer?

_____

12. Does the president like reporters (*reporteros*)?

_____

26 PRETERITE (simple past)

Study the verb endings for the preterite (*el pretérito*) of the -**ar** verbs and then do the exercises.

-AR Verbs

cantar (to sing)	-ar
yo canté	yo -é
tú cantaste	tú -aste
Ud. cantó	Ud.-ó
él, ella cantó	él, ella -ó
nosotros cantamos	nosotros -amos
Uds. cantaron	Uds. -aron
ellos, ellas cantaron	ellos, ellas -aron

- Note that the *nosotros* form is exactly like the one for the present indicative. The context clarifies the meaning.

A. Write the preterite (*el pretérito*).

1. hablar-yo _____
2. estudiar-yo _____
3. mirar-yo _____
4. bailar-tú _____
5. terminar-tú _____
6. comprar-tú _____
7. esperar-él _____
8. entrar-él _____
9. pronunciar-ella _____
10. contestar-Ud. _____
11. cantar-nosotros _____
12. practicar-nosotros _____
13. mirar-ellos _____
14. entrar-ellas _____
15. terminar-Uds. _____
16. bailar-nosotros _____

17. comprar-él _____

18. contestar-yo _____

19. estudiar-tú _____

20. entrar-Uds. _____

B. Change from present to preterite.

1. Yo hablo español. _____

2. Tú miras la televisión. _____

3. Usted canta una canción. _____

4. Él baila muy bien. _____

5. Ella termina la lección. _____

6. Ustedes esperan el autobús. _____

7. Ellos estudian el español. _____

8. Yo pronuncio muy bien. _____

9. Carlos habla italiano. _____

10. Linda estudia el francés. _____

11. Luis y María miran la televisión. _____

12. Los señores compran un coche. _____

13. Pancho y yo estudiamos en casa. _____

14. Pedro y yo cantamos muy mal. _____

15. Tú y Roberto estudian el portugués. _____

16. Usted y Conchita miran la televisión. _____

-ER and *-IR* Verbs

-er	-ir
comer (to eat)	**vivir** (to live)
yo com**í**	yo viv**í**
tú com**iste**	tú viv**iste**
Ud. com**ió**	Ud. viv**ió**
él, ella com**ió**	él, ella viv**ió**
nosotros com**imos**	nosotros viv**imos**
Uds. com**ieron**	Uds. viv**ieron**
ellos, ellas com**ieron**	ellos, ellas viv**ieron**

- The endings for the -**er** and -**ir** verbs are the same.

- Note that the ending for the third person for the -**er** and -**ir** verbs is -**ió**; in the -**ar** group it is -**ó.**
- The *nosotros* form for the -**er** group is slightly different from the *nosotros* in the present: *comimos* vs. *comemos* respectively.

C. Write the preterite.

1. escribir-yo _____
2. abrir-yo _____
3. recibir-yo _____
4. comer-tú _____
5. salir-tú _____
6. abrir-tú _____
7. beber-él _____
8. asistir-él _____
9. vivir-ella _____
10. comer-Ud. _____
11. aprender-nosotros _____
12. salir-nosotros _____
13. comprender-ellos _____
14. comer-ellas _____
15. vivir-Uds. _____
16. recibir-nosotros _____
17. abrir-él _____
18. salir-yo _____
19. asistir-tú _____
20. aprender-ellas _____

D. Change from present to preterite.

1. Yo como mucho. _____
2. Tú vives en Los Ángeles. _____
3. Usted escribe muchas cartas. _____
4. Yo abro las ventanas. _____
5. Tú comes mucho. _____
6. Usted sale a las dos. _____
7. Usted vive en Las Vegas. _____
8. Usted bebe el café. _____

9. Nosotros comemos mucho. _____

10. Nosotros escribimos mucho. _____

11. Nosotros salimos temprano. _____

12. Ustedes viven en España. _____

13. Ustedes beben la cerveza. _____

14. Ellos abren los libros. _____

15. Ustedes abren las puertas. _____

16. Ellos conocen a Luisa. _____

IRREGULAR PRETERITES

dar	hacer	ser/ir
yo di	yo hice	yo fui
tú diste	tú hiciste	tú fuiste
Ud. dio	Ud. hizo	Ud. fue
él, ella dio	él, ella hizo	él, ella fue
nosotros dimos	nosotros hicimos	nosotros fuimos
Uds. dieron	Uds. hicieron	Uds. fueron
ellos, ellas dieron	ellos, ellas hicieron	ellos, ellas fueron

- There are many irregular verbs in the preterite. In this section you are learning three of them.
- *Ser* & *ir* have exactly the same forms. The context clarifies the meaning.
- Remember that *hacer* means <u>to do</u> or <u>to make</u>, but is also used with many idiomatic expressions.

SPELLING CHANGES

- The preterite of *ver* does not have any accent marks: *vi, viste, vio, vimos, vieron*
- Verbs in *-car*, *-gar*, and *-zar* make a spelling change in the first person:
    - pagar- pagué, pagaste, pagó, pagamos, pagaron
    - buscar- busqué, buscaste, buscó, buscamos, buscaron
    - empezar- empecé, empezaste, empezó, empezamos, empezaron
- The third person of *creer* and *leer* changes the "i" into a "y"
    - creer- creí, creíste, creyó, creímos, creyeron
    - leer- leí, leíste, leyó, leímos, leyeron

Preterite

- *-Ar* and *-er* stem-changing verbs do not make changes in the preterite:
    pensar- pensé, pensaste, pensó, pensamos, pensaron
    volver- volví, volviste, volvió, volvimos, volvieron*

E. Write the preterite.
1. ver-Ud. _____
2. buscar-yo _____
3. volver-ella _____
4. dar-nosotros _____
5. ir-tú _____
6. llegar-yo _____
7. hacer-ellos _____
8. leer-él _____
9. dar-Ud. _____
10. ser-nosotras _____
11. pensar-ellas _____
12. creer-tú _____
13. empezar-yo _____
14. ser-Uds. _____
15. ver-ella _____
16. ir-nosotros _____

F. Change from present to preterite.
1. Yo llego tarde. _____
2. Ud. va a México. _____
3. Ellos son inteligentes. _____
4. Tú crees en Santa Claus. _____
5. Yo empiezo a comprender. _____
6. Nosotros vemos a los chicos. _____
7. Uds. dan muchos regalos. _____
8. Ella hace muchos favores. _____
9. Tú piensas en inglés. _____
10. Ud. vuelve aquí. _____
11. Nosotros vamos al laboratorio. _____
12. Yo busco a mis amigos. _____

---

*You will study stem-changing verbs in the preterite in another section.

Preterite

G. Review. Write the preterite.

	yo	tú	U.d, él, ella	nosotros	Uds.
1. cantar					
2. comer					
3. salir					
4. ir					
5. hacer					
6. creer					
7. pagar					
8. empezar					

H. Review of preterite.

1. mandar-Ud. _____

2. vivir-yo _____

3. comer-ellas _____

4. hacer-tú _____

5. escribir-nosotros _____

6. empezar-yo _____

7. pronunciar-ellos _____

8. dar-él _____

9. cenar-yo _____

10. salir-tú _____

11. ver-Ud. _____

12. ser-nosotros _____

13. aprender-Uds. _____

14. recibir-ella _____

15. estudiar-yo _____

16. ir-ellos _____

Preterite

17. terminar-Ud. _____

18. asistir-tú _____

19. creer-yo _____

20. pagar-Uds. _____

I. Review. Translate.

  1. I speak Spanish at home, but yesterday I spoke French.

_____

  2. We danced until two a.m.

_____

  3. The students went to class on time, but the teacher arrived late.

_____

  4. My father called me last week from Spain.

_____

  5. The secretary wrote a long letter.

_____

  6. Where did you (*fam.*) buy your car?

_____

  7. I did not do anything last week.

_____

  8. Did you (*pl.*) sell your Spanish books last year?

_____

  9. Luis left his house early this morning.

_____

10. Where did you (*form.*) learn Italian?

_____

11. I saw a good movie last night.

_____

Preterite

12. She read a long book.

_____

13. At what time did you (*form.*) return home yesterday?

_____

14. We gave our dad a watch for his birthday.

_____

15. He believed that she practiced math at the party.

_____

16. I paid 50 dollars for my Spanish book.

_____

27 IRREGULAR PRETERITES

The following verbs are irregular in the preterite. They all use the same endings: **e, iste, o, imos, ieron**. Study their forms and then do exercise A.

estar-estuv	**poder**-pud	**poner**-pus	**querer**-quis	**saber**-sup
estuve	pude	puse	quise	supe
estuviste	pudiste	pusiste	quisiste	supiste
estuvo	pudo	puso	quiso	supo
estuvimos	pudimos	pusimos	quisimos	supimos
estuvieron	pudieron	pusieron	quisieron	supieron

tener-tuv	**venir**-vin	**decir**-dij	**traer**-traj	**haber**
tuve	vine	dije	traje	**hubo** (there
tuviste	viniste	dijiste	trajiste	was, there
tuvo	vino	dijo	trajo	were)
tuvimos	vinimos	dijimos	trajimos	
tuvieron	vinieron	dijeron	trajeron	

- As you have noticed, the irregularities of the preceding verbs consist of the root and the first and third persons which do not have a written accent mark. You have also noticed that the ending for the third person plural of **decir** and **traer** is **-eron**, rather than **-ieron**.
- The preterites of **saber, conocer, querer, poder** have different meanings from those of their infinitives:

saber:	Yo sé hablar ruso.	I know how to speak Russian.
	Yo supe la verdad.	I found out the truth.

conocer:	Conocemos a Pedro.	We know Pedro.
	Conocimos a Luisa.	We met Luisa (made Luisa's acquaintance).

poder:	Podemos venir aquí mañana.	We can come here tomorrow.
	Pudimos venir aquí ayer.	We could (and did) come here yesterday (we managed).

querer:	Quieren aprender español.	They want to learn Spanish.
	Quisieron aprender español.	They tried to learn Spanish.
	No quisieron aprender español.	They refused to learn Spanish.

A. Write the preterite.

1. venir-yo _____
2. tener-yo _____
3. saber-yo _____
4. querer-tú _____
5. poner-tú _____
6. estar-tú _____
7. poder-él _____
8. decir-él _____
9. traer-ella _____
10. estar-Ud. _____
11. poder-nosotros _____
12. poner-nosotros _____
13. querer-ellos _____
14. saber-ellas _____
15. tener-Uds. _____
16. venir-nosotros _____
17. decir-tú _____
18. traer-yo _____
19. estar-él _____
20. poder-Uds. _____

B. Review. Write the preterite.

1. traer-Ud. _____
2. poder-yo _____
3. poner-ellas _____
4. decir-tú _____
5. querer-nosotros _____

Irregular Preterites

C. Review. Translate.

1. I met an interesting person last week.

_____

2. The students came to class on time.

_____

3. Did you (*pl.*) find out all about it?

_____

4. My parents refused to buy me a car.

_____

5. Where were you (*form.*) last night?

_____

6. Who told you (*fam.*) that?

_____

7. I put cream and sugar in my coffee, but I didn't put any liquor.

_____

8. We brought Mercedes flowers at the hospital.

_____

9. She had a bad day yesterday.

_____

10. I did not say anything.

_____

11. He was in school last week.

_____

12. We did not come here yesterday.

_____

Irregular Preterites

13. She tried to call me two hours ago.

_____

14. They brought wine to our party.

_____

15. There was a problem with his car.

_____

28 STEM-CHANGING PRETERITES

Stem-Changing Preterites

- *-Ar* and *-er* stem-changing verbs (*verbos que cambian la raíz*) do not make a stem change in the preterite:

  pensar- present: *pienso, piensas,* etc. *volver*: *vuelvo, vuelves,* etc.

          preterite: *pensé, pensaste,* etc.   *volví, volviste,* etc.

- *-Ir* stem-changing verbs make a change in the preterite but only in the third person singular and plural.

pedir (i, i)* (ask)	servir (i, i) (serve)	preferir (ie, i) (prefer)	sentirse (ie, i) (feel)
pedí	serví	preferí	sentí
pediste	serviste	preferiste	sentiste
pidió	sirvió	prefirió	sintió
pedimos	servimos	preferimos	sentimos
pidieron	sirvieron	prefirieron	sintieron

vestirse (i, i) (get dressed)	divertirse (i, i) (have a good time)	conseguir (i, i) (get, obtain)	despedirse** (i, i)(say good-bye)
vestí	divertí	conseguí	despedí
vestiste	divertiste	conseguiste	despediste
vistió	divirtió	consiguió	despidió
vestimos	divertimos	conseguimos	despedimos
vistieron	divirtieron	consiguieron	despidieron

---

*The two vowels in parenthesis indicate the stem changes in the present and in the preterite respectively.

**"Despedir" means "to fire" someone from a job.

Stem-Changing Preterites

seguir(i, i) (follow)	reírse (i, i) (laugh)	sonreír (i, i) (smile)	morir*** (ue, u) (die)	dormir (ue, u) (sleep)
seguí	reí	sonreí	morí	dormí
seguiste	reíste	sonreíste	moriste	dormiste
siguió	rió	sonrió	murió	durmió
seguimos	reímos	sonreímos	morimos	dormimos
siguieron	rieron	sonrieron	murieron	durmieron

A. Write the preterite.

1. morir-él _____

2. despedirse-yo _____

3. reírse-ella _____

4. conseguir-nosotros _____

5. divertirse-Uds _____

6. seguir-ellas _____

7. preferir-Ud. _____

8. pedir-tú _____

9. dormir-yo _____

10. divertirse-Ud. _____

11. despedirse-ellos _____

12. sonreír-nosotros _____

13. morir-ellas _____

14. vestirse-Uds. _____

15. servir-Luisa _____

16. sentirse-nosotros _____

17. seguir-Ud _____

18. dormirse-tú _____

***"Morir" is used primarily in the third person—**murió, murieron**. The other forms—**morí, moriste, morimos**— can be used in a fugurative sense.

Stem-Changing Preterites

19. conseguir-yo _____

20. pedir-Uds. _____

B. Review. Write the preterite.

1. vestirse-él _____

2. morir-ella _____

3. despedirse-Uds. _____

4. seguir-nosotros _____

5. dormirse-ellos _____

6. reírse-ella _____

C. Review. Translate.

1. We fell asleep at nine p.m.

_____

2. My father died two years ago.

_____

3. Luis had a good time at the party.

_____

4. Maria got a new job five months ago.

_____

5. I did not ask you (*fam.*) for money.

_____

6. He got dressed in ten minutes.

_____

7. They felt bad yesterday.

_____

8. The waiter served us good tamales.

_____

9. We laughed a lot in class.

_____

10. She said good-bye and left.

_____

11. They smiled when he served them coffee.

_____

12. My grandfather died last year.

_____

13. We followed all the directions.

_____

14. I slept many hours.

_____

29 DOUBLE OBJECT PRONOUNS

If two object pronouns are used in the same sentence, the indirect precedes the direct. Both pronouns will go before the conjugated verb.

> Luis **me** compra el regalo. Luis **me lo** compra.
> El profesor **nos** da los exámenes. El profesor **nos los** da.
> La doctora **te** dice la verdad. La doctora **te la** dice.

A. Use double object pronouns (*dos pronombres juntos*).

> **example**: Uds. me dicen la verdad. Uds. **me la** dicen.

1. Yo te mando tarjetas. _____
2. Ud. me canta la canción._____
3. Los chicos te prestan el dinero._____
4. María y tú nos sirven el pastel. _____
5. Nosotros te pedimos el favor._____
6. Uds. me hacen las preguntas. _____
7. Mis amigos me compran la cerveza._____
8. El secretario nos escribe las cartas._____
9. Yo te explico la gramática. _____
10. Conchita te trae el vino._____

If both direct and indirect begin with the letter **"l"**, the indirect changes to **"se"**.

- *El camarero **le** sirve la comida al cliente.*
- *El camarero ~~le~~ **la** sirve. El camarero **se la** sirve (**a él**).*
- *Nosotros **les** mandamos cartas a nuestros amigos.*
- *Nosotros **se las** mandamos (a ellos).*

Since this "*se*" may thus be the result of "*le*" (to you, to him, to her) or "*les*" (to them, to you pl.), at times it's necessary to clarify its meaning by adding *a él, a ella, a Ud., a ellos, a ellas, a Uds.* at the end.

B. Use double object pronouns.

> **example:** Nosotros le abrimos la puerta al doctor.
> Nosotros **se la** abrimos.

Double Object Pronouns

1. Yo le sirvo café a mi novia. _____

2. Uds. le dicen la verdad al sicólogo. _____

3. Nosotros le traemos los paquetes a Ud. _____

4. Luisa les manda el cheque a sus hijos. _____

5. Las chicas les prestan el dinero a sus amigos. _____

6. Tú le haces el favor al profesor. _____

7. Linda y yo les cantamos canciones mexicanas a los turistas.

_____

8. La doctora le explica el problema al paciente.

_____

9. Los estudiantes les recomiendan buenos restaurantes a Uds.

_____

10. El presidente no le dice mentiras a Ud.

_____

C. Answer in Spanish.
   example: *¿Ud. me da el dinero? Sí, (yo) se lo doy (a Ud.).*

1. ¿Ud. me compra la cerveza?

_____

2. ¿Me escribe Ud. la carta?

_____

3. ¿Me presta Ud. su coche?

_____

4. ¿Me manda flores Ud.?

_____

5. ¿Ud. me sirve la comida?

_____

D. Answer in Spanish.
   example: *¿Tú me das el dinero? Sí, (yo) te lo doy.*

1. ¿Tú me explicas la lección?

_____

2. ¿Me mandas tarjetas?

_____

3. ¿Tú me sirves el pastel?

_____

Double Object Pronouns

4. ¿Me pides el dinero?

_____

5. ¿Tú me cantas las canciones?

_____

6. ¿Me prestas tu maleta?

_____

E. Answer in Spanish.

example: *¿Ud. nos dice la verdad? Sí, (yo) se la digo (a Uds.).*

1. ¿Ud. nos dice mentiras?

_____

2. ¿Nos sirve Ud. la comida?

_____

3. ¿Ud. nos explica las lecciones?

_____

4. ¿Nos manda Ud. regalos?

_____

5. ¿Ud. nos compra la cena?

_____

F. Answer in Spanish.

example: *¿Ud. le dice la verdad a la doctora? Sí, (yo) se la digo (a ella).*

1. ¿Ud. le explica el problema al doctor?

_____

2. ¿Ud. le guarda el asiento a Pedro?

_____

3. ¿Le dice Ud. mentiras al sicólogo?

_____

4. ¿Le presta Ud. dinero a su hermano?

_____

5. ¿Le hace Ud. el favor a la chica?

_____

G. Answer in Spanish.

> **example**: *¿Ud. les dice la verdad a los chicos? Sí, (yo) se la digo (a ellos).*

1. ¿Ud. les da el dinero a los pobres?

_____

2. ¿Les compra Ud. la ropa a sus padres?

_____

3. ¿Tú les escribes poemas románticos a los chicos?

_____

4. ¿Les traes cerveza a tus profesoras?

_____

5. ¿Ud. les sirve café a los invitados?

_____

6. ¿Ud. les manda cheques a sus parientes?

_____

Double Object Pronouns with Infinitives

Double object pronouns can be attached to an infinitive or be placed in front of the conjugated verb. When the pronouns are attached, an accent mark will be placed on the vowel before the "**r**' of the infinitive.

> Yo **te los** quiero dar. Yo quiero dár**telos**
>
> Ellos **me las** pueden escribir. Ellos pueden escribír**melas**.
>
> Nosotros **se lo** vamos a mandar. Nosotros vamos a mandár**selo**.

H. Make the substitutions following the model.

> **example**: *Yo quiero comprarle un regalo a Ud.* <u>Yo se lo quiero comprar/ Yo quiero comprárselo a Ud</u>.

1. Los estudiantes quieren escribirme las cartas.

_____

_____

2. Nosotros deseamos hacerte el favor.

_____

_____

3. Tú vas a prestarnos tu coche.

_____

_____

4. Acabo de mandarles el cheque a mis primas.

_____

_____

5. Ellos te pueden comprar el coche nuevo.

_____

_____

6. Yo no quiero traerles cerveza a los niños.

_____

_____

I. Answer in Spanish.

> **example**: *¿Ud. me quiere dar el dinero? Sí, (yo) se lo quiero dar (a*
> *Ud.)/ Sí, yo quiero dárselo (a Ud.).*

1. ¿Ud. me desea comprar la cerveza?

_____

_____

2. ¿Me va a escribir Ud. la carta?

_____

_____

3. ¿Tú me vas a explicar la lección?

_____

_____

4. ¿Me puedes mandar tarjetas?

_____

_____

5. ¿Ud. va a decirnos mentiras?

_____

_____

6. ¿Quiere Ud. traerles cerveza a sus amigos?

_____

_____

Double Object Pronouns

7. ¿Vas a explicarles el problema a tus padres?

_____

_____

J. Review. Answer using double object pronouns.

1. ¿Ud. me pide el dinero?

_____

2. ¿Nos cantas canciones mexicanas?

_____

3. ¿Quieren Uds. darnos el sombrero?

_____

4. ¿Los alumnos le traen regalos al profesor?

_____

5. ¿Yo les sirvo cerveza a Uds.?

_____

6. ¿Deseas comprarme los regalos?

_____

7. ¿Ud. nos explica la gramática?

_____

8. ¿El doctor les dice la verdad a los pacientes?

_____

9. ¿Me prestas tu coche?

_____

10. ¿Ud. me va a mandar tarjetas postales?

_____

11. ¿Uds. le dicen mentiras a su papá?

_____

12. ¿Me abren Uds. la ventana?

_____

13. ¿Nosotros le hacemos preguntas al presidente?

_____

14. ¿Puedes escribirme el poema?

_____

K. Review. Translate.

1. The money? I am giving it to him.

_____

2. Our new boat? We have just lent it to her. (*two ways*)

_____

_____

3. The long letters? They are writing them to me.

_____

4. The expensive gift? She is sending it to us.

_____

5. Our problem? We are explaining it to you (*form.*).

_____

6. The final exam? The instructor can give it to you (*fam.*) tomorrow.

_____

_____

7. The enchiladas? Are you (*pl.*) serving them to her?

_____

8. His French dictionaries? He is lending them to me.

_____

9. The package? She is going to send it to us.

_____

_____

10. The situation? I am going to describe (*describir*) it to you (*form.*).

_____

_____

11. The Italian wine? They are not bringing it to you (*fam.*)

_____

12. Lies? She is not telling them to him.

_____

13. The Lexus? We are buying it for them.

_____

14. The money for my trip to Tahiti? I am asking them for it.

_____

15. The romantic poems? They cannot write them for us.

_____

_____

30 IMPERFECT

The imperfect (*el imperfecto*) is a past tense that is used in a number of situations. For the moment, concentrate on learning the forms of the imperfect and keep in mind that it is used for repeated actions and descriptions in the past.

-AR

cantar
yo cant**aba**
tú cant**abas**
Ud. cant**aba**
él, ella cant**aba**
nosotros cant**ábamos**
Uds.cant**aban**
ellos, ellas cant**aban**

Note that the ending *-aba* is used for *yo, Ud., él,* and *ella.*

A. Write the correct form of the imperfect (**-AR**).

1. Yo cantaba todos los días.

   Ud._____

   Tú _____

   Ellas _____

2. Tú mirabas la tele todas las noches.

   Uds. _____

   Él _____

   Nosotros _____

3. Los chicos estudiaban en la tarde.

   María _____

   Tú _____

   El doctor y yo _____

Imperfect

4. Yo no hablaba francés.

Ella _____

Nosotras _____

Uds. _____

5. Ella arreglaba su coche.

Yo _____

Tú _____

Los profesores y yo _____

6. Ellos buscaban a sus amigos.

Nosotros _____

Conchita _____

Pedro y tú _____

7. Yo estaba bien.

Mercedes _____

Tú _____

Ud. y su papá _____

8. Ellos tocaban el piano.

Ella _____

Tú _____

Uds. _____

La enfermera _____

9. Yo me acostaba temprano.

Tú _____

Ellos _____

Nosotros _____

Ud. _____

10. Ellos se levantaban tarde.

Nosotras _____

Tú _____

Sus hermanos _____

-ER	-IR
comer	vivir
yo comía	yo vivía
tú comías	tú vivías
Ud. comía	Ud. vivía
él, ella comía	él, ella vivía
nosotros comíamos	nosotros vivíamos
Uds. comían	Uds. vivían
ellos, ellas comían	ellos, ellas vivían

Note that the endings for *-er* and *-ir* verbs are the same and that the "*i*" always has an accent mark.

B. Write the correct form of the imperfect (**ER + IR**).

1. Ellas vivían en San Diego.

   Tú _____

   Nosotros _____

   La criada _____

2. Tú no hacías nada.

   Yo _____

   Mi papá _____

   Sus amigos _____

3. Ellas leían la revista.

   Uds. _____

   Yo _____

   Carlos y yo _____

   Tú _____

4. Ella bebía mucho vino.

   Nosotros _____

   El estudiante _____

   Mi familia _____

   Tus parientes _____

5. Tú insistías en hablar inglés.

   Ellos _____

   El secretario _____

   Las señoras _____

Imperfect

6. Ella se dormía en clase.

Yo _____

Ellos _____

Nosotras _____

El chico rubio _____

7. Yo me sentía mal.

Tú _____

Ella _____

Nosotros _____

Ellos _____

8. Ella se vestía rápidamente.

Nosotros _____

Tú _____

Yo _____

Los chicos _____

9. Yo comprendía el subjuntivo.

Uds. _____

La señorita _____

Francisco y yo _____

Luisa y su hermana _____

10. Tú escribías las cartas.

Nosotros _____

Los secretarios _____

Mi tío _____

Irregular Imperfects

- There are no stem-changing verbs in the imperfect.
- The following are the only irregular verbs in the imperfect.

ir	ser	ver
yo iba	yo era	yo veía
tú ibas	tú eras	tú veías
Ud., él, ella iba	Ud., él, ella era	Ud., él, ella veía
nosotros íbamos	nosotros éramos	nosotros veíamos
Uds., ellos, ellas iban	Uds., ellos, ellas eran	Uds., ellos, ellas veían

C. Review. Write the correct forms of the imperfect.

	yo, Ud., él, ella	tú	nosotros	Uds.
1. estudiar				
2. tomar				
3. llegar				
4. entender				
5. recibir				
6. vender				
7. ver				
8. ir				
9. ser				

D. Review. Translate. (Most verbs in this exercise need to be translated with the imperfect).

1. On Saturdays, I would always watch television.

_____

2. When Conchita was twelve, she used to play the piano.

_____

3. As a child, Luis used to have dinner early.

_____

4. You (*fam.*) were distracted in class because you were thinking about your girlfriend.

_____

5. Pedro was sick.

_____

6. Many people used to read a lot.

_____

7. While we were going to school, other people were going to the office.

_____

8. It was one p.m. when I had lunch.

_____

9. They were ordering dinner when we were going in the restaurant.

_____

10. When he was in elementary school, he would return home at 2 p.m.

_____

11. My father used to smoke.

_____

12. Our grandparents had big cars.

_____

13. I used to drink milk.

_____

14. Her son used to wake up at 1 a.m. when he was a baby.

_____

15. You (*pl.*) were happy because all of your family was home for Christmas.

_____

Narrating in the Past
Preterite vs. Imperfect

> **TIPS:** *1. **Make sure** you know the regular and irregular forms for the preterite and the imperfect.*
> *2. **Study** the sections on the use of the imperfect and preterite in your textbook.*

- The preterite is used for completed actions in the past:
  Comí la enchilada (a las seis) <u>I ate the enchilada (at six)</u>.
- When the speaker wishes to stress that the action may not have been completed (we don't see the end, we can't put a specific time on the action), the imperfect is used:
  - *Comía la enchilada cuando Pedro llegó a mi casa.*
    <u>I was eating (i.e., in the middle of eating) when Pedro arrived at my house.</u>
    Pedro's arrival interrupted the eating (the act of eating may or may not have been carried out).
- The imperfect is used for descriptions and to set the stage or provide background for the preterite:
  - *Hacía sol y yo estaba contento. Por eso decidí ir a la playa.*

It was sunny and I was happy. That's why I decided to go to the beach.

- *Pedro estaba enfermo y por eso no vino a clase.*
  Pedro was sick and that's why he did not come to class. (It's not clear for how long he was sick; emphasis on condition and preparation for "no vino")

- The imperfect gives the background or explanation for something that took place:

  - *Como (since) llovía, yo no salí de casa.* Since it was raining, I did not go out of my house.

  - *Comió mucho porque tenía hambre.* She ate a lot because she was hungry.

- Verbs such as *estar, ser, tener,* are used more often in the imperfect rather than the preterite because they are "static," i.e., they suggest descriptions, states, or conditions rather than actions. When these verbs are used in the preterite, there is always a specific reference to time (expressed or implied) by the speaker.

  Pedro estuvo enfermo tres días.
  Pedro was sick for three days.

- Other verbs are considered "action" verbs —eat, go, come, write, etc.—and are normally used in the preterite because they suggest completed actions.

  Francisco vino a clase. Luis y María llegaron a las siete.
  Francisco came to class. Luis and Maria arrived at seven.

- These action verbs can be used in the imperfect to express habitual actions. In English, these imperfects are translated with "*used to* or *would* + a verb":

  Yo cenaba a las siete todas las noches. I used to (would) have dinner at six every night.

- Action verbs can also be used to translate the English past progressive, i.e., *was* or *were* +_____ing:

  Ella estudiaba cuando él llegó. She **was studying** when he arrived.

Words Associated with the Imperfect

todos los días, todos los meses, todos los martes... siempre, generalmente, de vez en cuando, mientras, de niño, de joven.

Words Associated with the Preterite

ayer, anoche, el mes pasado, el año pasado, ...una vez, de repente (all of a sudden).

E. Imperfect or preterite? Write I or P in the space provided.

1. It's used in descriptions. _____
2. It's used to tell time. _____
3. It's used to express incomplete actions. _____
4. It's used to express completed actions. _____
5. It's used to translate *was* or *were* + __*ing*. _____
6. It's used with "static" verbs such as "tener," "ser," "estar" etc. _____
7. It's used with "static" verbs when they are clearly identified with a specific time reference. _____
8. It's used with action verbs to express repeated, habitual actions. _____
9. It's used with action verbs to express completed actions. _____

DIFFERENT MEANINGS OF PRETERITE VS. IMPERFECT

conocer- to know: *Yo conocí a Luis.* <u>I **met** Luis.</u>
            Yo conocía a Pedro. <u>I **knew** Pedro.</u>
saber-to know: *Yo supe la verdad.* <u>I **found out** the truth.</u>
            Yo sabía la verdad. <u>I **knew** the truth.</u>
poder- to be able: *Yo pude hacer la tarea.* <u>I **managed** to do the homework</u> (could *and* did).
            Yo podía hacer la tarea. <u>I **had the ability** to do the homework</u> (I am not saying whether I did it or not).
querer-to want: *Yo quise comer veinticinco tacos.* <u>I **tried** to eat twenty-five tacos</u> (I acted on my desire).

Yo quería comer veinticinco tacos. **I had the desire** to eat twenty-five tacos (I am not saying whether I made the attempt, it was just a wish).

*Yo **no** quise comer veinticinco tacos.* **I refused** to eat twenty-five tacos.

tener-to have: *Tuve una fiesta.* **I gave** a party (planned and had).

Tenía varios amigos. **I had** many friends (ongoing situation, no beginning or end).

tener que- have to, must: *Tuve que ir a casa.* **I had** to go home (**did go**).

Tenía que ir a casa. **I was supposed** to go home (no end result implied, maybe I did or didn't go).

deber: have to, must: *Debí ir a casa.* **I had** to go home (**did go**).

Debía ir a casa. **I was supposed** to go home (no end result implied, maybe I did or didn't go).

pensar-to think: *Pensé que él era inocente.* It **dawned** on me that he was innocent.

Pensaba que él era inocente. **I thought** that he was innocent (ongoing opinion, no beginning or end implied).

estar- to be: *Estuve en casa todo el día.* I was home all day.

Estaba en casa, pero luego decidí ir al cine. I was home, but then I decided to go to the movies.

ser- to be: *Fui buen estudiante.* I was a good student (from beginning to end of a time period expressed or suggested, i.e., high school, elementary school, college).

Era buen estudiante, pero luego empecé a estudiar poco y..... I was a good student, but then I began not to study very much and ......

F. Translate.

1. Pedro was twelve years old when he arrived in California.

_____

2. When we met the instructor (*fem.*), we already knew her daughter.

_____

Imperfect

3. I had to go to work (*did go*).

_____

4. They could buy the new car, but they decided to wait until next year.

_____

5. Where were you (*form.*) the entire week?

_____

6. He was supposed to be here at nine.

_____

7. At the beginning (*al comienzo*), she didn't know anything about his problems. Later, when she found out about them, she tried to help him.

_____

_____

8. We tried to read the entire novel.

_____

9. When Luis was in elementary school (*la escuela elemental*), he was a good student.

_____

10. The children refused to eat the carrots (*zanahorias*).

_____

MODELS

Read sections I & II and try to understand why the preterite (*el pretérito*) or the imperfect (*el imperfecto*) is used.

I

1. Cuando yo <u>tenía</u> ocho años, <u>vivía</u> con mis tres hermanos y mis padres en Santa María, donde yo <u>asistía</u> a una escuela pública.

2. Mi papá <u>trabajaba</u> en Union Sugar y mi mamá <u>trabajaba</u> en Marian Hospital.

3. Una vez, mis padres <u>viajaron</u> a Alemania. Mis hermanos y yo nos <u>quedamos</u> (we stayed) con mis tíos. Todo <u>iba</u> bien hasta que un domingo por la tarde, mi hermana menor se <u>rompió</u> (broke) una pierna. Cuando mis padres <u>supieron</u> del accidente, <u>querían</u> volver, pero mis tíos les aseguraron (assured them) que no <u>era</u> necesario.

4. Un día cuando mi hermana mayor <u>aprendía</u> a manejar el coche, ella <u>chocó</u> (crashed) con la puerta del garaje. No <u>volvió</u> a manejar por cuatro años.

Imperfect

II

El miércoles pasado, cuando Carlos Gómez Márquez se <u>levantó</u>, <u>dijo</u> que no se <u>sentía</u> bien. No <u>pudo</u> dormir toda la noche y le <u>dolía</u> (hurt) el pecho (chest). Inmediatamente <u>hizo</u> una cita con el médico. El Sr. Gómez <u>estaba</u> muy nervioso porque <u>temía</u> algo serio, como un ataque al corazón. El doctor lo <u>examinó</u> y le <u>dijo</u> que no <u>era</u> nada grave, que solamente <u>estaba</u> muy cansado, que <u>debía</u> dormir más y comer menos. El doctor le <u>dio</u> unas vitaminas y pastillas (pills) para dormir. Y cuando el Sr. Gómez <u>regresó</u> a casa, ya se <u>sentía</u> mucho mejor.

G. Circle the preterite or the imperfect.

Hizo/hacía[1] buen tiempo. Los pajaritos (little birds) *cantaban/cantaron*[2] en el parque. Luis *estaba/estuvo*[3] muy contento porque *tenía/tuvo*[4] una cita con una chica muy bonita. Él *esperó/esperaba*[5] dos horas, pero la chica no *aparecía/apareció*[6]. Luego, esa misma noche Luis *veía/vio*[7] a la chica en un restaurante con otro muchacho. Él *pensaba/pensó*[8] que el otro era su nuevo novio y no le *quiso/quería*[9] hablar. Ella lo *llamaba/llamó*[10] y le *explicaba/explicó*[11] que el otro chico *era/fue*[12] su hermano. Luis *se sentó/se sentaba*[13] con ellos y los tres *charlaban/charlaron*[14] (chat) por largo rato. Finalmente Luis y la chica *planearon/planeaban*[15] otra cita y él *salía/salió*[16] del restaurante muy contento.

H. Review. Fill in the correct form of the preterite or the imperfect.

Mercedes y Jackie (ser)[1] _____ muy buenas amigas. Ellas (vivir)[2] _____ en Los Ángeles y (estudiar)[3] _____ en la misma escuela primaria. Todos los días ellas (ir)[4] _____ a la escuela y (pasar)[5] _____ mucho tiempo juntas después de las clases.

    En 1984 ellas (graduarse)[6] _____ de la escuela secundaria y (ir)[7] _____ a universidades diferentes. Mercedes (asistir)[8] _____ a una universidad en Costa Rica donde ella (conocer)[9] _____ a un joven español. Ella (casarse)[10] _____ con él y ahora ellos viven en España.

    Jackie (ir)[11] _____ a una universidad francesa. Allí ella (conocer)[12] _____ a un joven de Alemania. Los dos ahora viven en Estados Unidos donde enseñan matemáticas en una escuela secundaria.

Aunque (although) Mercedes y Jackie viven en países diferentes, todavía son buenas amigas porque ellas recuerdan los años que ellas (pasar)[13] _____ en Los Ángeles durante su infancia.

I. Review. Translate.

It was seven o'clock when I finally left home. It was cold, but there were many people who were going to work. At seven thirty I arrived at the office. My boss was angry. I told him that it was not a good idea to get angry because it's possible to get sick. He answered that I was his secretary and not his psychologist. It's true. Next time that he gets angry I am not going to give him any advice. And maybe I am going to find another boss who understands me!

_____

_____

_____

_____

_____

_____

_____

_____

_____

_____

_____

_____

31 *POR* AND *PARA*

The prepositions (*las preposiciones*) **por** and **para** translate into English as "for." Yet, they are used in different situations. You have already encountered many examples with the usage of these two prepositions. Try to keep them in mind. However, a few generalizations can be useful.

     Para is normally used for some type of destination or direction in which an action is aimed at—a place, a goal, or a recipient. **Por** is used to express the motive or reason behind an action rather than the goal ahead. This distinction accounts for many of the usages of the two prepositions. Many other usages are not easily explained. **Por**, especially, has a variety of uses that fall into the category of idiomatic phrases.

     Por and **para** can be translated with "for," but depending on the context they may be translated with nearly every other preposition.

     What follows will help you learn **por** and **para** better.

Usage of *Por*

Por is used to translate

- *by, by means of*

    Van a Europa por avión. They are going to Europe by plane.
    Me habla por teléfono. She speaks to me on the phone.
- *through, along*

    Le gusta pasear por la playa. He likes to stroll on the beach.
- *around*

    Por aquí. Around here.
- *during, in* (time of day)

    Estudiamos por la mañana y por la noche.
    We study in the morning and at night.
- *because, due to*

    Estoy aquí por la cita con el doctor.
    I am here because of the appointment with the doctor.
- *in exchange of*

    Pagaron 15.000 dólares por el coche.

They paid 15,000 thousand dollars for the car.
- *for someone's sake*

    Lo hice por ti porque te quiero.

    I did it for you because I love you.
- *duration* (often omitted)

    Trabajó en Costa Rica (por) tres años.

    S/he worked in Costa Rica for three years.
- *yet to be done*

    Tienen la composición por escribir.

    They have yet to write the composition.
- *to be in favor of*

    Están por la paz.

    They are in favor of peace.
- *after, to get something*

    Van a la tienda por pan.

    They are going to the store to get bread.
- *no matter how much*

    Por mucho que lo repita, no lo comprenden.

    No matter how much I repeat it, they won't understand it.
- *as a substitute*

    Hoy trabajo por la profesora porque está enferma.

    Today I work for the teacher because she is sick.
- *per* (*per hour, per week, per month*)

    Trabajan cuarenta horas por semana.

    They work forty hours per week.
- *times* or *by* (in multiplication or division)

    cinco por cinco-five times five

    cien dividido por veinte-a hundred divided by twenty
- *by* (in the passive construction)

    El pastel fue hecho por Mercedes. The cake was made by Mercedes.

Por is also used in the following expressions

    por Dios-for heaven's sake

    por ejemplo-for example

    por eso-that's why

    por favor-please

por fin-finally

por lo general-generally

por lo menos-at least

por primera vez-for the first time

por última vez-for the last time

por si acaso-just in case

¡por supuesto!-Of course!

¿por qué?-why?

porque-because

estar por- to be for (in favor)

preguntar por- to ask about

preocuparse por- to worry about

Usage of *Para*

Para is used to translate

- *in order to*

    Estudian mucho para sacar buenas notas.

    They study hard (in order) to get good grades.

- *destined for, to be given to*

    El regalo es para Ud. The gift is for you.

    Preparó una cena especial para mí.

    He prepared a special dinner for me.

- *for* (a deadline, specified future time)

    Hagan la tarea para mañana. Do the homework for tomorrow.

    La cita es para el jueves. The date is for Thursday.

- *for* (toward, in the direction of)

    Salió para Portugal. He left for Portugal.

- *for* (purpose, to be used for)

    El dinero es para la comida. The money is for the food.

    Es una clase para niños. It's a class for children.

- *for* (as compared to others, in relation to others)

    Para el presidente la economía anda bien.

    For the president, the economy is going alright.

    Para un francés, habla muy bien el italiano.

    For a Frenchman, he speaks Italian very well.

- *for* (in the employ of)

    Trabajan para la universidad. They work for the university.
- *to be about to*

    Están para comer. They are about to eat.
- *for ever*

    Nunca regresaremos allí. Nos fuimos para siempre.
    We will never return there. We left for ever.

A. Fill in *por* or *para.*

1. Ellos lo hicieron _____ ella porque la quieren mucho.

2. Viene _____ mí más tarde.

3. Tienes que traerle la composición _____ el miércoles.

4. Su hijo estudia _____ ingeniero.

5. Estos regalos son _____ Uds.

6. Nunca viaja _____ avión porque tiene miedo.

7. Caminan _____ la Calle Bolívar.

8. Tu cita es pasado mañana _____ la tarde.

9. No vino a la escuela _____ el mal tiempo.

10. Nos ofrecieron ochocientos dólares _____ el coche.

11. Fue a la fiesta _____ divertirse.

12. ¿_____ qué no me llamas después de cenar?

13. Fueron a la tienda _____ leche.

14. No necesitas mucho dinero _____ comer en McDonald's.

15. ¿Cuándo sale Ud. _____ Francia?

16. Hablan portugués muy bien _____ ingleses.

17. Trabajó _____ una tienda de ropa.

18. La cucharita es _____ comer helado.

19. Voy a estar en la oficina _____ las diez.

20. El criminal entró _____ la ventana y salió _____ puerta.

21. Si ganamos la lotería, vamos a viajar _____ toda Europa.

22. —¿Vienes a la fiesta?

    ¡_____ supuesto!

23. _____ allí no hay más restaurantes.

24. La enchilada fue hecha _____ su papá.

25. Estudió muchos años _____ doctor y _____ fin se graduó.

26. _____ mucho que ellos me lo repitan, no lo recordaré.

27. Este bolígrafo rojo es _____ corregir composiciones.
28. Siete _____ nueve son sesenta y tres.
29. Estudié francés _____ cinco semestres.
30. Vinieron aquí _____ la entrevista.

B. Review. Translate.

1. I lost my keys. That's why I went in through the window.

_____

2. She never travels by ship. It's too expensive.

_____

3. When are you (*fam.*) leaving for Spain?

_____

4. They were walking along the beach when I saw them.

_____

5. We went to the bank for money.

_____

6. The doctor is going to be late for my appointment.

_____

7. The kids did not go to school because of the rain.

_____

8. She did it for him because she loves him.

_____

9. For Friday, study (*pl.*) Chapter 8.

_____

10. They run very fast for old people.

_____

11. We are bringing our umbrellas just in case.

_____

Por and Para

12. I always have a good breakfast early in the morning.

_____

13. Conchita paid 200,000 dollars for her house.

_____

14. He works for a Mexican company.

_____

15. Mercedes is studying to become a doctor.

_____

16. The book was written by a famous author.

_____

17. Those gifts are for her. These are for you (*pl.*).

_____

18. For the Spanish teacher *por* and *para* are easy.

_____

19. We study many hours per week for that class.

_____

20. They are taking math for the last time.

_____

32 FAMILIAR COMMANDS

The familiar **negative** commands (*mandatos familiares negativos*) are very easy. You just add an "**s**" to the formal commands.

Formal Commands	Familiar Negative Commands
¡Hable Ud.!	¡No hables tú!
¡Coma Ud.!	¡No comas tú!
¡Escriba Ud.!	¡No escribas tú!
¡Diga Ud.!	¡No digas tú!
¡Sepa Ud.!	¡No sepas tú!

Remember that unlike in English, the subject pronouns are sometimes expressed with commands in Spanish. In that case, they will be placed after the verb.

A. Change from formal to **negative** familiar commands.

1. ¡Empiece Ud. a estudiar! _____
2. ¡Cene Ud. a las seis! _____
3. ¡Trabaje Ud. mucho! _____
4. ¡Regrese Ud. temprano! _____
5. ¡Practique Ud. toda la lección! _____
6. ¡Almuerce Ud. con su esposo! _____
7. ¡Pague Ud. la cuenta! _____
8. ¡Juegue Ud. a la lotería! _____
9. ¡Saque Ud. la foto! _____
10. ¡Esté Ud. listo para el examen! _____
11. ¡Vuelva Ud. aquí mañana! _____
12. ¡Duerma Ud. ocho horas! _____
13. ¡Pida Ud. el dinero! _____
14. ¡Repita Ud. la oración! _____
15. ¡Diga Ud. la verdad! _____
16. ¡Ponga Ud. el dinero en el banco! _____

17. ¡Sea Ud. buena! _____

18. ¡Dé Ud. dinero a los pobres! _____

19. ¡Vaya Ud. al laboratorio! _____

20. ¡Sepa Ud. los verbos irregulares! _____

21. ¡Traiga Ud. su perro a la clase! _____

22. ¡Salga Ud. con la chica rica! _____

Familiar Affirmative Commands

Familiar **affirmative** commands (*mandatos familiares afirmativos*) of regular verbs have the same endings as the 3rd person of the present indicative tense.

3rd person of present indicative	familiar affirmative commands
Ella habl**a**	¡Habla tú!
Él cant**a**	¡Canta tú!
Él escrib**e**	¡Escribe tú!
Ella com**e**	¡Come tú!

B. Give advice to you friend Luis (-**ar**, -**er**, -**ir**).

     example: *Luis no canta bien.* ¡Luis, canta bien!

1. Luis no escucha a su papá. _____

2. " " habla francés. _____

3. " " mira la televisión. _____

4. " " prepara la cena. _____

5. " " toca el piano. _____

6. " " estudia las matemáticas. _____

7. " " llega a tiempo. _____

8. " " termina la tarea. _____

****

9. " " escribe la composición. _____

10. " " lee la novela. _____

11. " " trae el libro a la escuela. _____

12. " " duerme bastante. _____

Familiar Commands

Irregular Familiar Affirmative Commands

decir-di	salir-sal
hacer-haz	ser-sé
ir-ve	tener-ten
poner-pon	venir-ven

- Note that *ir* and *ver* have the same affirmative command. The context clarifies the meaning.

  Ve a la escuela. Go to school.

  Ve esa película. See that movie.

C. Give advice to Luis. Change from affirmative to negative commands.

example: *¡Luis, habla francés!* ¡Luis, no hables francés!

¡Luis, come poco! ¡Luis, no comas poco!

¡Luis, sal ahora! ¡Luis, no salgas ahora!

1. ¡Luis, bebe la leche! _____

2. ¡Luis, compra el coche! _____

3. ¡Luis, escribe el poema! _____

4. ¡Luis, mira el programa! _____

5. ¡Luis, canta en portugués! _____

****

6. ¡Luis, di la verdad! _____

7. ¡Luis, pon limón en el vino! _____

8. ¡Luis, ven aquí ahora! _____

9. ¡Luis, haz la tarea! _____

10. ¡Luis, ve al laboratorio!_____

11. ¡Luis, sé bueno! _____

12. ¡Luis, ten paciencia! _____

13. ¡Luis, ve el programa! _____

Familiar Commands and Pronouns

- The position of direct and indirect object pronouns with the formal and familiar command forms is the same. With negative commands, the pronouns are placed in front of the verb.

  *¡No comas el taco. No **lo** comas!*

  *¡No le hables a Pancho. No **le** hables!*

Familiar Commands

- With affirmative commands, the pronouns are attached to the verb and a written accent will also be necesary.

¡Compra tú los regalos. Cómpralos!

*¡Llámanos! ¡Escríbenos! ¡Háblame!**

The accent mark will be placed on the stressed syllable of the verb form (the syllable where the voice goes up).

D. Change from affirmative to negative. Note the position of the pronouns and that of the written accent mark. Also note the change in verb form from affirmative to negative.

examples: ¡Cántala! ¡No la cant**es**!

¡Escríbeles a ellos! ¡No les escrib**as** a ellos!

1. Fúmala. _____

2. Escríbela. _____

3. Ábrelos. _____

4. Léelos. _____

5. Tómalas. _____

6. Enséñalo. _____

7. Búscanos. _____

8. Sírvela. _____

9. Repítela. _____

10. Piénsalo. _____

11. Empiézala. _____

12. Ciérralo. _____

E. Write the accent mark (*el acento escrito*) on the appropriate vowel.

1. escribele	2. sacala	3. repitelas	4. sirvela
5. bebelo	6. arreglala	7. compralos	8. comela
9. llamanos	10. buscalo	11. cantala	12. hablale

---

* The accent mark is not necessary with familiar commands that consist of one syllable only: *Di. Dime. Haz. Haznos.* If two pronouns are added to these verbs, then the accent mark is necessary. *Dímelo. Háznosla.*

Reflexive Pronouns and Familiar Commands

Reflexive pronouns, just like object pronouns, are attached to the affirmative forms and placed before the negative ones.

F. Change from affirmative to negative. Keep in mind the change in vowels.

    examples: ¡Siéntate tú! ¡No te sientes!

                 ¡Acuéstate tú! ¡No te acuestes!

1. ¡Levántate! _____

2. ¡Báñate! _____

3. ¡Quítate la chaqueta! _____

4. ¡Lávate! _____

5. ¡Aféitate! _____

6. ¡Despiértate! _____

*****

    example: ¡Vístete tú! ¡No te vistas!

7. ¡Diviértete! _____

8. ¡Vístete! _____

9. ¡Duérmete! _____

Familiar Commands and Double Object pronouns

G. Change from affirmative to negative.

    examples: *¡Cómpramela tú!*   ¡No me la compres tú!

                 ¡Escríbemela tú!   ¡No me la escribas tú!

1. ¡Cántamela tú! _____

2. ¡Mándamela tú! _____

3. ¡Dímela tú! _____

4. ¡Tráemela tú!_____

5. ¡Sírvenoslas tú! _____

6. ¡Házmelo tú! _____

7. ¡Prométenoslo tú! _____

8. ¡Pídenoslo tú!_____

H. Review. Write the formal and familiar commands.

	Ud.	Uds.	Tú (*negative*)	Tú (*affirm.*)
1. estudiar				
2. escribir				
3. empezar				
4. volver				
5. hacer				
6. poner				
7. ir				
8. venir				
9. traer				

I. Review. Translate. Use familiar commands (*mandatos familiares*).

1. Buy the car. Buy it now.

_____

2. Go to school. Go everyday.

_____

3. Don't go out tonight.

_____

4. Come here on Friday.

_____

5. Don't sell your house. Don't sell it now.

_____

6. Sell your motorcycle. Sell it today.

_____

7. Get on the plane.

_____

8. Start your lessons. Start them now.

_____

9. Put the pen on the table. Don't put it in your coffee.

_____

10. Sleep seven hours, but don't sleep in class.

_____

11. Don't look for us today. Look for us tomorrow.

_____

12. Order the steak and eat it.

_____

13. Don't bring us your problems. Don't ever bring them to us.

_____

14. Take two aspirins and <u>don't</u> call me in the morning.

_____

15. Think about it.

_____

16. Prepare the dinner for Mary. Prepare it for her.

_____

17. Send us your address. Send it to us soon.

_____

18. Explain the grammar to the students, but don't explain it to them in Greek (_griego_).

_____

33 SUBJUNCTIVE

The subjunctive (*el subjuntivo*) is used when the main clause (*la cláusula principal*) (usually the first part of the sentence) contains a verb indicating wish, possibility, doubt, denial, or emotion. The verb of the dependent clause (*la cláusula subordinada*) (usually the second part of the sentence) will be in the subjunctive. In this section you will be learning the forms for the present subjunctive (*el presente de subjuntivo*) and its usage with some verbs of volition (wish or desire) —*querer* and *desear, etc.*— in the main clause. The rest of the usage will be dealt with later.

The forms for the present subjunctive are:

-AR	-ER	-IR
cantar	**comer**	**escribir**
yo cante	yo coma	yo escriba
tú cantes	tú comas	tú escribas
Ud., él, ella cante	Ud., él, ella coma	Ud., él, ella escriba
nosotros cantemos	nosotros comamos	nosotros escribamos
Uds., ellos, ellas canten	Uds., ellos, ellas coman	Uds., ellos, ellas escriban

A. Write the present subjunctive (-AR verbs). The first form of numbers 1-4 is given to you. You should be able figure out the rest easily.

1. Los chicos quieren que yo cante en francés.
   "   "   "   " Ud. _____
   "   "   "   " nosotros _____

2. Tu papá no quiere que tú estudies en la noche.
   " " " " " ellos _____
   " " " " " nosotras _____

3. Deseamos que Uds. enseñen filosofía.
   "   " ella _____
   "   " tú _____

4. No queremos que Uds. fumen aquí.
   "   "   " él _____
   "   "   " las chicas _____

5. Mi mamá no quiere que yo (comprar) _____ mucha ropa.

   "   "   "   "   " Uds. _____

   "   "   "   "   " Pedro y yo _____

6. ¿Desean Uds. que nosotros (regresar) _____ mañana?

   "   "   " yo _____

   "   "   " mi papá _____

7. Yo no quiero que tú (llevar) _____ esa corbata fea.

   " " "   " Uds. _____

   " " "   " mi hijo _____

8. ¿Quieres que yo (mirar) _____ el programa contigo?

   "   " ellos _____

   "   " nosotros _____

9. No queremos que Ud. (bailar) _____ en la clase.

   "   "   " tú _____

   "   "   " la profesora _____

10. ¿Quieren Uds. que yo los (llamar) _____ más tarde?

   "   "   " la doctora los _____

   "   "   " los secretarios los _____

B. Write the present subjunctive (-ER & -IR). The first form of numbers 1 & 2 is given to you. You should be able to figure out the rest easily.

1. Los doctores desean que Ud. coma menos.

   "   "   "   " tú _____

   "   "   "   " nosotros _____

2. Yo no quiero que Uds. vivan en Casmalia.

   " " "   " mis amigos _____

   " " "   " ella _____

3. Nosotros queremos que tú escribas la carta en portugués.

   "   "   " Uds. _____

   "   "   " él _____

4. Los profesores quieren que yo (aprender) _____ los verbos.

   "   "   "   " Uds. _____

   "   "   "   " nosotros _____

5. Francisca quiere que nosotros (asistir) _____ al
   concierto de Madonna.

   "   "   " los alumnos _____

   "   "   " Luisa y yo _____

6. ¿Quieren que yo (abrir) _____ el regalo ahora?

   "   " nosotros _____

   "   " Pedro _____

7. Su hermano no desea que tú (insistir) _____ mucho.

   "   "   "   "   " yo _____

   "   "   "   "   " ellas _____

8. Mi papá no quiere que yo (vender) _____ el coche.

   "   "   "   "   " mi hermano y yo _____

   "   "   "   "   " tú _____

9. La profesora de literatura quiere que nosotros (leer) _____
   toda la novela.

   "   "   "   "   "   " los estudiantes _____

   "   "   "   "   "   " mi esposa _____

10. Nosotros no deseamos que Uds. (beber) _____ tequila en
    el laboratorio.

    "   "   "   " ella _____

    "   "   "   " los profesores _____

IRREGULAR VERBS
Review the irregular verb forms before doing exercise "C"
Stem-Changing Verbs

e>ie	o>ue	e>i
cerrar-cierre	almorzar-almuerce	pedir-pida
empezar-empiece	dormir-duerma	servir-sirva
pensar-piense	poder-pueda	repetir-repita
preferir-prefiera	volver-vuelva	vestir-vista
perder-pierda		
querer-quiera		
Stem change in all except the "nosotros" form; EXCEPTION: prefiramos	No change in the "nosotros" form; EXCEPTION: "dormir"-durmamos	Stem change in all forms

Verbs with Spelling Changes

Verbs in -CAR	Verbs in -GAR	Verbs in -ZAR
buscar-bus**que**	pagar-pa**gue**	empezar-empie**ce**
sacar-sa**que**	llegar-lle**gue**	comenzar-comien**ce**
practicar-practi**que**	jugar-jue**gue**	abrazar-abra**ce**
Spelling change in all forms	Spelling change in all forms; *jugar* also makes stem change	Spelling change in all forms; *empezar* and *comenzar* also make stem change

Irregular Verbs Based on the First Person of the Present Indicative

DECIR	HACER	OíR	PONER	SALIR
diga	haga	oiga	ponga	salga
digas	hagas	oigas	pongas	salgas
digamos	hagamos	oigamos	pongamos	salgamos
digan	hagan	oigan	pongan	salgan
TENER	**TRAER**	**VENIR**	**VER**	**CONOCER**
tenga	traiga	venga	vea	conozca
tengas	traigas	vengas	veas	conozcas
tengamos	traigamos	vengamos	veamos	conozcamos
tengan	traigan	vengan	vean	conozcan

Other Irregular Verbs

DAR	ESTAR	IR	SABER	HABER
dé	esté	vaya	sepa	haya
des	estés	vayas	sepas	(there is OR
demos	estemos	vayamos	sepamos	there are)
den	estén	vayan	sepan	

C. Write the correct form of the present subjunctive (irregular verbs).

1. Ellos quieren que tú (pagar) _____ la cerveza.

" " " nosotros _____

" " " las chicas _____

2. Nosotros no deseamos que Uds. (empezar) _____ a llorar.

" " " " María _____

" " " " Luisa y tú _____

Subjunctive

3. Quiero que Uds. (conocer) _____ a mi hermano
Pedro.

    "   "   tu novia _____

    "   "   la hermana del arquitecto _____

4. ¿Quieres que yo te (dar) _____ el número de teléfono del
chico moreno?

    "   "   el profesor te _____

    "   "   mis amigos te _____

5. No desean que Ud. (saber) _____ todos sus secretos.

    "   "   "   tú _____

    "   "   "   nosotros _____

6. El esposo de Conchita no quiere que ella (poner) _____
azúcar en el café.

    "   "   "   "   "   "   nosotros _____

    "   "   "   "   "   "   Uds. _____

7. No queremos que tú nos (decir) _____ mentiras.

    "   "   "   ellas nos _____

    "   "   "   la hermana de Linda nos _____

8. No quiere que (haber) _____ problemas en su fiesta.

9. Mis amigos quieren que nosotros (oír) _____ la nueva
canción.

    "   "   "   "   nuestros primos_____

    "   "   "   "   su papá _____

10. Los padres de Luisa quieren que ella (estar) _____ en
casa a las diez.

    "   "   "   "   "   "   nosotros _____

11. ¿Deseas que yo te (traer) _____ el café ahora?

    "   "   nosotros te _____

    "   "   ellos te _____

12. ¿Quieren Uds. que nosotros les (hacer) _____ el favor a
Uds.?

    "   "   "   yo les _____

    "   "   "   nuestra mamá les _____

13. El jefe desea que Ud. (comenzar) _____ el trabajo
pronto.

    "   "   "   "   nosotros _____

    "   "   "   "   tú _____

Subjunctive

14. Los profesores no quieren que Ud. (dormir) _____ en
                                                                clase.

    "   "   "   "   " Ricardo y yo _____

15. Werner desea que Uds. (poder) _____ hablar bien.

    "   "   " ella _____

    "   "   " nosotras _____

16. La mamá de Pancho no desea que yo (salir) _____ con
                                                                su hija.

    "   "   "   "   "   "   " tú _____

    "   "   "   "   "   "   " nosotros _____

17. Quiero que Uds. (tener) _____ paciencia.

    "   " la doctora _____

18. El profesor quiere que los alumnos (venir) _____ a clase a
                                                                tiempo.

    "   "   "   " nosotros _____

19. Los alumnos quieren que yo (ver) _____ el programa
                                                                esta noche.

    "   "   "   " nosotros _____

20. Yo no deseo que Ud. (buscar) _____ a mi hermano.

    " "   "   " Luisa y María _____

21. Queremos que tú (ir) _____ al cine con nosotros.

    "   " los chicos _____

22. Mis padres no quieren que yo (perder) _____ el
                                                dinero en Las Vegas.

    "   "   " "   " nosotros _____

23. El novio de María desea que Uds. (almorzar) _____ en
                                                                el restaurante.

    "   "   "   "   "   " la doctora _____

    "   "   "   "   "   " nosotros _____

24. ¿Quieres que nosotros (jugar) _____ al fútbol?

    "   " ellas _____

25. No quiero que mi papá me (encontrar) _____ aquí.

    "   "   " sus hermanas me _____

D. Review. Translate.

1. They want me to speak Spanish now.

_____

Subjunctive

2. I want you (*form.*) to write me every week.

_____

3. The children want us to send them gifts.

_____

4. His cousin does not want you (*fam.*) to call him at three a.m.

_____

5. Teachers want students to study a lot.

_____

6. Doctors don't want their patients to smoke.

_____

7. We want you (*pl.*) to go to Mexico by plane.

_____

8. My mom wants me to be able to play the guitar.

_____

9. I don't want you (*pl.*) to drink a lot.

_____

10. The teacher wants us to bring the books to class.

_____

11. His girlfriend does not want him to go out with other women.

_____

12. Her husband does not want her to see her ex-boyfriend.

_____

13. They want me to know how to swim.

_____

14. Our doctor wants us to exercise one hour a day.

_____

15. I want you (*fam.*) to meet my daughter.

_____

SUBJUNCTIVE: USAGE

- The present tense you learned in the first part of your course is part of the **indicative mood**, which also includes a number of other tenses, such as the preterite, imperfect, future, etc. All the indicative tenses have one thing in common: they all indicate **facts**—in the present, past, or future.

- **The subjunctive**, of which you have learned the forms for the present tense, indicates things that may or may not happen. The subjunctive deals with possibilities, things we want or hope other people will do.

Subjunctive

- Compare the following sentences:
  1. *I ate three enchiladas.*
  2. *My father wants me to eat twenty enchiladas.*

In example # 1, it is obvious how many enchiladas I ate. In example # 2, it's not. I may decide to eat all the twenty my father wants me to eat or I may decide not to eat them.

- The present subjunctive is used when the **main clause** (usually the first part of the sentence) ("My father wants" in example #2 above) **contains a verb indicating wish, desire, doubt, denial, possibility, need, or emotion.** The verb in the main clause acts as a "trigger" for the subjunctive.
  a) *Quiero que Ud. trabaje.* <u>I want you to work</u>.
  b) *Deseo que tú cantes.* <u>I wish that you would sing.</u>
  c) *Dudo que tengas un millón de dólares.* <u>I doubt you have a million dollars.</u>
  d) *Me alegro que estés aquí.* <u>I am glad that you are here</u>.

- The verb in the subjunctive denotes something that may or may not happen (exception: when the "trigger" is an emotion; in example d), the action expressed by the subjunctive is indeed true).

Subjunctive with Verbs of Influence

The subjunctive is used with verbs of influence, i.e., verbs meaning that someone wants someone else to do something. These verbs include *desear, querer, insistir, necesitar, decir, mandar* (order), *pedir, permitir, preferir, prohibir, recomendar, etc.* Generalizations of influence such as *es necesario, es importante, es preciso* (it's necessary), *es urgente, es preferible*, etc., also trigger the subjunctive.

E. Fill in the correct form of the present subjunctive. As you do the exercise, pay special attention to the "trigger" for the subjunctive which is given to you in bold face.

1. El profesor **quiere** que los estudiantes (llegar) _____ a tiempo.
2. Los padres **insisten** en que los hijos (regresar) _____ a casa temprano.
3. Mi doctor no **recomienda** que yo (comer) _____ muchas hamburguesas.

4. El general **manda** que los soldados (soldiers) (ir) _____ al frente (front).

5. El cliente **pide** que la camarera le (traer) _____ la comida pronto.

6. La ley (law) no **permite** que tú (robar) _____.

7. La mamá de Luis **prefiere** que él (hacerse) (become) _____ doctor.

8. Nosotros **deseamos** que Uds. (saber) _____ toda la verdad.

9. **Es importante** que el presidente (explicar) _____ la situación política.

10. **Es urgente** que yo (tomar) _____ el examen final.

11. **Es preferible** que Ud. (salir) _____ de casa temprano.

12. **Es preciso** que yo (aprender) _____ el subjuntivo.

Subjunctive with Expressions of Emotion

Expressions of emotion also trigger the subjunctive. Some of these include *ojalá* (I hope), *esperar* (to hope), *tener miedo* (to be afraid), *temer* (to fear), *estar contento, estar triste, gustar, sentir* (to regret), *sorprender* (to be surprised), *molestar* (to be bothered). Generalizations of emotion such as *es terrible, es lástima* (it's a pity), *es extraño* (it's strange), *¡qué extraño!* (How strange!), *es bueno, es malo, es mejor*, also trigger the subjunctive.

F. Fill in the correct form of the present subjunctive. As you do the exercise, pay special attention to the "trigger" for the subjunctive which is given to you in bold face.

1. **Ojalá** que mi papá (ganar) _____ la lotería.

2. **Es lástima** que yo no (poder) _____ comprar un BMW.

3. **Tenemos miedo** que el profesor nos (dar) _____ una prueba mañana.

4. **Me sorprende** que (haber) _____ muchos alumnos en la clase de las ocho de la mañana.

5. A mi mamá le **gusta** que nosotros (sacar) _____ "A" en la clase de matemáticas.

6. **¡Qué extraño** que la profesora (llegar) _____ temprano a veces!

7. Nos **gusta** que la economía (ser) _____ mejor.

8. **Es malo** que muchas personas (fumar) _____.

9. El presidente **tiene miedo de** que los periodistas (reporters) le
(hacer) _____ preguntas difíciles.

10. Los periodistas **esperan** que el presidente les (dar) _____
una entrevista exclusiva.

11. **Sentimos** mucho que tu hermano (estar) _____ en el
hospital.

12. **Es terrible** que yo siempre (tener) _____ mucha tarea.

Subjunctive with Expressions of Doubt and Denial

Expressions of doubt, denial, and possibility such as *dudar* (to doubt), *no estar seguro, no creer,* *negar* (ie) (to deny), *no es verdad***, *no es seguro* (it's not a sure thing),*(no) es posible, (no) es imposible, (no) es probable, (no) es improbable,* also trigger the subjunctive.

G. Fill in the correct form of the present subjunctive. As you do the exercise, pay special attention to the "trigger" for the subjunctive which is given to you in bold face.

1. **No creen** que yo (poder) _____ comer la pizza entera.
2. Yo **no estoy seguro** que Ud. (levantarse) _____ a las tres
de la mañana.
3. **No es verdad** que el presidente de México (ser) _____
Plácido Domingo.
4. **Es posible** que los doctores (ganar) _____ poco dinero,
pero no es probable.
5. **Niegan** que tú (comprender) _____ el subjuntivo.
6. **Dudamos** que los políticos (decir) _____ la verdad.
7. **Es improbable** que Uds. (ir) _____ a Nueva York en
bicicleta.
8. **Es imposible** que nosotros (leer) _____ Hamlet en tres
minutos.
9. **Dudo** que Hillary Clinton (comer) _____ en McDonald's.
10. **Es posible** que Bill Clinton (querer) _____ comer en
McDonald's.

Subjunctive After Non-Existing and Uncertain Antecedents

The subjunctive is also used when the antecedent is either indefinite or non-existent:

> *Hay restaurantes donde sirven huevos para el desayuno.*
> <u>There are restaurants where they serve eggs for breakfast.</u>
> (antecedent exists=indicative)

> *No hay restaurantes donde sirvan pizza para el desayuno.*
> <u>There are no restaurants where they serve pizza for breakfast.</u>
> (antecedent non-existent)

> *Busco un* * *doctor que **sepa** hablar portugués.*
> <u>I am looking for a doctor who knows how to speak Portuguese.</u>
> (uncertain)

> *Busco al doctor que **sabe** hablar español.*
> <u>I am looking for the doctor who knows how to speak Spanish.</u>
> (doctor exists)

H. Fill in the correct form of the present subjunctive.

1. Necesito un compañero que (venir) _____ a Europa conmigo.
2. En esta universidad no hay ningún profesor que (saber) _____ hablar japonés muy bien.
3. ¿Hay algunas blusas que a ti te (gustar) _____?
4. No conocemos a nadie que (poder) _____ completar el examen final en diez minutos.
5. Buscamos unos libros que (tener) _____ información sobre Portugal.
6. ¿Hay alguien en el garaje que (poder) _____ arreglar carros extranjeros?
7. No hay nadie en mi clase de francés que (hablar) _____ chino.
8. No conocen a nadie que (tocar) _____ el piano con los pies (feet).
9. ¿Tienes un amigo que (saber) _____ preparar comida rusa?
10. Los estudiantes necesitan un apartamento que (estar) _____ cerca de la universidad.

Subjunctive After Conjunctions

The following conjunctions of contingency or purpose will trigger the subjunctive.

> *antes de que* (before), *a menos que* (unless), *con tal de que* (provided that), *en caso de* (in case), *sin que* (without), *para que* (so that), *hasta que* (until).

---

* The personal "a" is not used if the person may not exist.

Subjunctive

Vengo al cine con tal que tú pagues los boletos.
I'll come to the movies provided you pay for the tickets.
Estudiamos mucho antes de que la profesora nos dé el examen.
We study a lot before the teacher gives us the exam.
No van a comprar el Porsche a menos que ganen la lotería.
They won't buy the Porsche unless they win the lottery.

Note that the events in subordinate clause have not taken place and may or may not take place. Also remember that if the subject does not change, the infinitive is used.

Preparo la cena para que Uds. coman.
I prepare dinner so that you may eat.
Preparo la cena para comer.
I prepare dinner so that I may eat.

I. Fill in the correct form of the present subjunctive. As you do the exercise, pay special attention to the "trigger" for the subjunctive which is given to you in bold face.

1. Es importante estudiar **antes de que** el profesor nos (dar) _____ el examen.

2. Hacemos el trabajo bien **con tal que** Uds. lo (explicar) _____ claramente.

3. Luisa va a llevar paraguas (umbrella) **en caso de que** (llover) _____.

4. Los padres pueden dormir hasta muy tarde **a menos que** el bebé los (despertar) (wake) _____.

5. Vamos al restaurante **antes de que** (cerrar) _____.

6. El camarero sirve la comida **para que** nosotros (comer) _____.

7. Llegan al cine **antes de que** la película (empezar) _____.

Subjunctive After Conjunctions of Time

The following conjunctions will trigger the subjunctive when the verb after them is aimed at the future. The idea is that the actions represented by the subjunctive may or may not happen.

cuando, después de, en cuanto (as soon as), *hasta que, tan pronto como* (as soon as).

Vamos a empezar la lección en cuanto llegue el profesor.
We are going to start the lesson as soon as the instructor arrives.
Tienen que esperar hasta que el camarero les traiga la comida.
They have to wait until the waiter brings them the food.

If the action after these conjunctions is in the past, the indicative will be used since these actions really took place, i.e., they are part of the indicative mood.

> *Comenzamos la lección en cuanto el profesor llegó.*
> <u>We began the lesson as soon as the teacher arrived.</u>

J. Fill in the correct form of the present subjunctive. As you do the exercise, pay special attention to the "trigger" for the subjunctive which is given to you in bold face.

1. Voy a comprar un coche nuevo **en cuanto** el banco me (prestar) _____ el dinero.

2. Vamos a pagar las cuentas **cuando** nosotros (recibir) _____ nuestro cheque.

3. Pedro va a graduarse **tan pronto como** él (terminar) _____ su tesis.

4. Van a cenar **después de** que el camarero les (traer) _____ la comida.

5. Mis padres van a esperar **hasta que** nosotros (regresar) _____ de nuestro trabajo.

6. Los turistas van a visitar muchos museos **en cuanto** ellos (llegar) _____ a Italia.

7. Nosotros vamos a contestar **tan pronto como** la profesora nos (preguntar) _____.

8. Voy a quedarme (stay) en casa **hasta que** no (llover) _____ más.

TIPS

1. When the subjunctive is used, the subjects of the two clauses are different.
2. The Spanish subjunctive can be expressed in English with an infinitive, an indicative, a subjunctive, a future, or a verb preceded by the auxiliary "may", depending on the meaning.
3. In many cases, the difference between the indicative and the subjunctive involves just a minor change in vowel. Compare:
- *Luis habla. Quiero que Luis hable.*
- *Pedro come. Mandamos que Pedro coma.*

K. Review. Write the correct form of the present subjunctive.

1. estudiar	yo		nosotros
2. vivir	Uds.		nosotros
3. leer	él		nosotros
4. querer	tú		nosotros
5. poner	ellas		nosotros
6. ir	yo		nosotros
7. preferir	ella		nosotros
8. jugar	Uds.		nosotros
9. servir	él		nosotros
10. saber	tú		nosotros
11. hacer	ellas		nosotros
12. mandar	yo		nosotros
13. comenzar	ella		nosotros
14. salir	Uds.		nosotros
15. dar	él		nosotros
16. venir	tú		nosotros

L. Review. Translate.

1. I don't want you (*fam.*) to arrive late.

_____

2. The doctor tells me not to smoke.

_____

3. It's important that we go on vacation.

_____

4. The tourists ask us to take (*llevar*) them to the airport.

_____

5. They are surprised that I can eat and speak at the same time (*al mismo tiempo*).

_____

6. The president is not happy that reporters want to know everything.

_____

7. How strange that there is an elephant in the swimming pool (*piscina*).

_____

8. It's terrible that the teacher always gives us homework.

_____

9. It's evident that you (*pl.*) finished your lessons.

_____

10. It's not true that doctors write clearly (*claramente*).

_____

11. It's impossible for my daughter to read a novel in thirty minutes.

_____

12. We don't know anyone who can speak French, Spanish, and German with his dog.

_____

13. Are you (*form.*) looking for the student who knows how to play the guitar?

_____

14. John's wife works so that he can study medicine at the university.

_____

15. The secretary comes to the office provided that his boss makes coffee in the morning.

_____

16. They are going to the bank as soon as it opens.

_____

17. She is going to wait until I arrive.

_____

18. We are sad that Conchita is in the hospital.

_____

19. It bothers me (*Me molesta*) that you (*fam.*) always ask me for money.

_____

20. My mother prohibits me to drive her Maserati.

_____

34 PRESENT PERFECT INDICATIVE

The present perfect indicative (*el presente perfecto de indicativo*) is formed with the present tense of *haber* and the past participle (*el participio pasado*).

Present Perfect
yo **he cantado**
tú **has cantado**
Ud. **ha cantado**
él, ella **ha cantado**
nosotros **hemos cantado**
Uds. **han cantado**
ellos, ellas **han cantado**

past participle		
-ar	-er	-ir
cantar-cant**ado**	comer-com**ido**	vivir-viv**ido**

- The present perfect is used in general as it is in English. Normally the time phrase you are considering is still open.

  Esta semana yo he comido en un restaurante tres veces.
  <u>This week I have eaten in a restaurant three times</u>. (I may eat again in a restaurant).
  La semana pasada yo comí en un restaurante tres veces.
  <u>Last week I ate in a restaurant three times</u>. (The week is over; no more opportunities).
- The past participle does not change.

A. Write the present perfect (*el presente perfecto*).

1. Yo he hablado mucho esta semana.

Tú _____

Ud. _____

Nosotros _____

Ellos _____

2. Uds. no han comido todavía.

Yo _____

Ella no _____

Luisa y yo no _____

Tú no _____

3. Nosotros no hemos mirado ese programa este mes.

Yo no _____

Tú no _____

Ud. no _____

4. Ellos han estudiado mucho, pero todavía necesitan estudiar más.

Ella _____

Tú _____

Nosotros _____

Yo _____

5. Luis no ha cantado mi canción favorita todavía.

Ellas no _____

Tú no _____

Ud. no _____

Pedro y tú _____

Irregular Past Participles

caer-caído	abrir-abierto	romper-roto
creer-creído	decir-dicho	ver-visto
leer-leído	escribir-escrito	volver-vuelto
oír-oído	hacer-hecho	resolver-resuelto
sonreir-sonreído	morir-muerto	cubrir-cubierto
traer-traído	poner-puesto	descubrir-descubierto

B. Write the presente perfect (*el presente perfecto*).

1. Yo nunca he cantado en japonés.

   Ellos nunca _____

2. Nosotros ya hemos visitado a nuestros padres.

   Tú ya _____

3. Ellas han buscado a sus amigos.

   Yo _____

4. Uds. han pedido muchos favores.

   Luis y yo _____

5. El doctor todavía no ha venido.

   Mis amigos _____

6. Ellos no han comido nunca en ese restaurante.

   Tú no _____

7. Nosotros ya hemos servido las bebidas.

   Mi mamá ya _____

8. Los chicos ya han aprendido el vocabulario.

   Ella ya _____

9. ¿Has leído todo el libro?

   ¿Ellos _____ ?

10. Han traído diccionarios aquí.

    Nosotros _____

11. Uds. no han creído esa historia.

    Yo no _____

12. Hemos oído algo interesante.

    Tú _____

13. He caído, pero no me he roto el brazo.

    Ella _____ pero no se _____

14. El restaurante todavía no ha abierto.

    Las tiendas _____

15. Ellos no han dicho nada.

    Nosotros no _____

16. No han hecho la tarea todavía.

    Yo no _____

17. ¿Has visto la nueva película?

    ¿Ellos _____ ?

Present Perfect Indicative

18. Todavía ella no ha vuelto a casa.

Todavía mis hijos _____

19. ¿Has escrito la composición?

¿Ellos _____ ?

20. Ya hemos resuelto el problema.

Ella ya _____

21. Uds. han descubierto todo.

Yo _____

22. El gato ya ha muerto tres veces.

Los gatos ya _____

C. Write the past participle (*el participio pasado*).

1. Pedro no ha (comprar) _____ su libro todavía.

2. Yo nunca he (estar) _____ en China.

3. Uds. han (visitar) _____ muchos museos.

4. Nosotros hemos (cerrar) _____ las ventanas.

5. Tú no has (tratar) _____ de resolver el problema.

6. Ella me ha (mandar) _____ muchas tarjetas.

7. Ya hemos (cenar) _____.

8. Uds. nunca han (manejar) _____ un Maserati.

9. Luis no ha (practicar) _____ los verbos todavía.

10. No hemos (nadar) _____ en el océano todavía.

****

11. Ellos no han (aprender) _____ los verbos irregulares.

12. Nosotros hemos (subir) _____ al piso número treinta.

13. ¿Te han (pedir) _____ dinero?

14. ¿Ha (conocer) _____ a alguna persona interesante?

15. ¿Todavía ellos no se han (ir) _____?

*****

16. Yo no he (hacer)_____ nada interesante esta semana.

Present Perfect Indicative

17. Uds. ya han (ver) _____ esa película.
18. Nosotros todavía no hemos (escribir) _____ el
    poema.
19. Ellos no han (oír) _____ el ruido.
20. María me ha (decir) _____ todo.
21. Tú no has (descubrir) _____ la verdad.
22. No hemos (volver)_____ al laboratorio.
23. El gato es muy viejo, pero todavía no ha (morir)
    _____.

24. Es un problema muy difícil, pero ella ya lo ha (resolver)
    _____.

25. Nunca hemos (traer) _____ nuestro perro a la clase.

D. Review. Write the correct form of the present perfect indicative.

1. mirar	yo		tú
2. cantar	él		nosotros
3. traer	Ud.		ellas
4. abrir	ellos		tú
5. hacer	él		Uds.
6. ver	nosotros		ella
7. servir	ellos		tú
8. caer	yo		Luisa
9. decir	él y tú		Uds.
10. poner	nosotros		ella

E. Review. Translate.

1. Have you (*fam.*) visited Japan yet?

   _____

2. Have they learned their lesson yet?

   _____

3. We have eaten in that restaurant many times.

   _____

4. He has bought a new car already.

   _____

Present Perfect Indicative

5. The doctor has not arrived yet.

_____

6. We have been to Mexico and Guatemala several times, but we
   have never been to Colombia.

_____

_____

7. He has already done many favors for us.

_____

8. I have not discovered the truth yet.

_____

9. Students have already learned many verbs.

_____

10. They have asked me for money.

_____

11. She has told him the story.

_____

12. Has your (*fam.*) father returned from Europe yet?

_____

13. I have always been a good student.

_____

14. My sons have already learned how to play the piano and the
    guitar.

_____

15. We have not opened our gifts yet.

_____

16. It's a difficult problem, but I think we have already solved it.

_____

17. He has fallen many times, but he has not broken anything yet.

_____

18. The tourists have written some cards, but have not written any
    letters yet.

_____

19. This month I have eaten in restaurants several times already.

_____

20. We have not spoken to her yet, but we want to do it soon.

_____

Present Perfect Indicative

35 PRESENT PERFECT SUBJUNCTIVE

- The present perfect subjunctive (*el presente perfecto de subjuntivo*) is formed with the present subjunctive of **haber** and the past participle.
- The present perfect subjunctive is used when the verb in the main clause "triggers" the subjunctive and the verb in the subordinate clause is in the past.

> *Dudo que él haya comido treinta tacos.* <u>I doubt that he ate thirty tacos.</u>
>
> *Dudo que el profesor ya haya preparado el examen final.*
> <u>I doubt that the teacher has already prepared the final exam.</u>

present perfect subjunctive

yo haya cantado
tú hayas cantado
Ud. haya cantado
él, ella haya cantado
nosotros hayamos cantado
Uds. hayan cantado
ellos, ellas hayan cantado

A. Write the correct form of the present perfect subjunctive (-AR verbs).

1. Dudan que yo haya hablado con el presidente ayer.

    "   "   tú _____

    "   "   Ud. _____

    "   "   nosotros _____

    "   "   ellos _____

2. No creen que Uds. hayan tomado tequila en el restaurante japonés.

    "   "   "   yo _____

    "   "   "   ella _____

    "   "   "   Luisa y yo _____

    "   "   "   tú _____

3. Les gusta que nosotros no hayamos mirado ese horrible programa anoche.

    "   "   " yo no _____

    "   "   " tú no _____

    "   "   " ellas no _____

    "   "   " Ud. no _____

4. No es verdad que ellos hayan estudiado mucho el semestre pasado.

    "   "   "   " ella _____

    "   "   "   " tú _____

    "   "   "   " nosotros _____

    "   "   "   " yo _____

5. Es posible que Luis haya cantado mi canción favorita en la fiesta.

    "   "   " ellas _____

    "   "   " tú _____

    "   "   " Ud. _____

    "   "   " Pedro y tú _____

B. Write the correct form of the present perfect subjunctive (regular and irregular). You may want to review the irregular past participles in the previous chapter before proceeding with this exercise.

1. Es posible que Pedro no (comprar) _____ el coche nuevo.

2. Dudan que yo (estar) _____ en China ayer.

3. No está seguro que Uds. (visitar) _____ muchos museos.

4. Me alegro que él (cerrar) _____ las ventanas.

5. Es posible que tú no (tratar) _____ de resolver el problema.

6. Niego que ella me (mandar) _____ muchas tarjetas.

7. Siento que sus hijas no (cenar) _____.

8. Es probable que Uds. nunca (manejar) _____ un Maserati.

9. Es malo que Luis no (practicar) _____ los verbos.

10. No es verdad que el profesor (nadar) _____ en el océano.

11. Es increíble que ellos no (aprender) _____ el presente.

Present Perfect Subjunctive

12. Dudan que nosotros (subir) _____ al piso número treinta en tres minutos.
13. Ojalá que ellos no te (pedir) _____ mucho dinero.
14. Es bueno que tú (conocer) _____ a muchas personas interesantes en tu viaje.
15. ¿Es posible que ellos no (ir) _____ a su clase?
16. Es lástima que yo no (hacer)_____ nada interesante esta semana.
17. Me alegro que Uds. (ver) _____ esa película mexicana el mes pasado.
18. No es verdad que nosotros no (escribir) _____ el poema.
19. Es imposible que ellos no (oír) _____ la explosión.
20. Dudan que María me (decir) _____ todos sus secretos.
21. No es posible que tú (descubrir) _____ toda la verdad.
22. Es malo que nosotros no (volver)_____ al laboratorio.

C. Review. Write the present perfect subjunctive (*el presente perfecto de subjuntivo*).

1. cenar	yo	nosotros
2. hablar	ellas	Ud.
3. comer	nosotros	tú
4. aprender	Uds.	María
5. decir	tú	ellos
6. hacer	Luis	tú
7. escribir	ellas	él
8. volver	tú	yo
9. ver	él	nosotros
10. conocer	yo	tú

D. Review. Translate.

1. They don't believe I have visited Japan many times.

_____

Present Perfect Subjunctive

2. It's good that they learned their lessons.

_____

3. It's not true that we ate in that awful restaurant five times.

_____

4. It's possible that he has bought a new car already.

_____

5. I don't think that the doctor arrived on time.

_____

6. We are glad that you (*form.*) have been to Mexico and Guatemala several times.

_____

7. They doubt that he has done many favors for me.

_____

8. It's impossible that they have not discovered the truth yet.

_____

9. She denies that students have already learned many verbs.

_____

10. It's a pity that he has asked me for money again.

_____

11. I hope they have told him the story.

_____

12. It's probable that her father returned from Europe.

_____

13. It's not true that I have been a bad student.

_____

Present Perfect Subjunctive

14. It's incredible that her sons learned how to play the piano and the guitar in three months.

_____

_____

15. They doubt that we have not opened our gifts yet.

_____

16. I hope that they solved their difficult problem.

_____

17. It's incredible that he fell many times and that he has not broken his legs (*piernas*).

_____

18. I am glad that the tourists have written some cards.

_____

TIP: *As you saw in section D, the present perfect subjunctive may translate in English as a simple past or in some cases as a present perfect.*

Present Perfect Subjunctive

36 FUTURE

In English, the future tense uses the helping verb "will" and the verb:

examples: I will go. You will study.

The future tense (*el futuro*) in Spanish is formed by using the infinitive as the stem and adding **é, ás, á, emos, án.**

Future

cantar	comer	escribir
yo cantaré	yo comeré	yo escribiré
tú cantarás	tú comerás	tú escribirás
Ud. cantará	Ud. comerá	Ud. escribirá
él, ella cantará	él, ella comerá	él, ella escribirá
nosotros cantaremos	nosotros comeremos	nosotros escribiremos
Uds. cantarán	Uds. comerán	Uds. escribirán
ellos, ellas cantarán	ellos, ellas comerán	ellos, ellas escribirán

- The endings for all three conjugations (**-ar, -er,** and **-ir**) are the same.
- The endings for the future tense are almost the same as those for the present tense of **haber** (*he, has, ha, hemos, han*) except that in the future the letter "**h**" is dropped.
- Some of the forms for the future tense resemble those of the imperfect subjunctive, except for the presence of accent marks in the future tense:

  hablara-hablará, cantaran-cantarán, estudiaras-estudiarás
- All the forms in the future have an accent mark except "*nosotros*".

A. Write the future (*el futuro*) (regular verbs).

1. Yo cantaré en francés el año próximo.

   Ud. _____

   Tú _____

   Ellas _____

2. Tú no mirarás la tele en el futuro.

Uds. _____

Él _____

Nosotros _____

3. Los chicos estudiarán mucho.

María _____

Tú _____

El doctor y yo _____

4. Yo hablaré chino en 2030.

Ella _____

Nosotras _____

La enfermera _____

Uds. _____

5. Ella arreglará su coche.

Yo _____

Tú _____

Los profesores y yo _____

6. Ellos buscarán a sus amigos.

Nosotros _____

Yo _____

Conchita _____

Pedro y tú _____

7. Yo estaré en España en el verano.

Mercedes _____

Tú _____

Las amigas _____

Ud. y su papá _____

8. Ellos tocarán el piano muy bien el año próximo.

Ella _____

Tú _____

Uds. _____

La enfermera _____

9. Yo me acostaré temprano el mes próximo.

Tú _____

Ellos _____

Nosotros _____

Ud. _____

10. Ellos se levantarán temprano.

Uds. _____

Nosotras _____

Tú _____

Sus hermanos _____

11. Ellas vivirán en la luna en 2050.

Yo _____

Tú _____

Nosotros _____

La criada _____

12. Uds. leerán poco en el futuro.

Ellos _____

Yo _____

Carlos y yo _____

13. Ella beberá mucho vino en Francia.

Nosotros _____

El estudiante _____

Mi familia _____

Tus parientes _____

14. Tú no insistirás en hablar inglés el año próximo.

Ellos _____

El secretario _____

Tú _____

Las señoras _____

15. Ella no se dormirá en clase.

Yo _____

Ellos _____

Nosotras _____

El chico rubio _____

Irregular Futures

The irregularities in these verbs occur in the stem. The endings are the same as those for regular futures.

decir-diré, dirás, etc.	saber-sabré, sabrás, etc.
hacer-haré, harás, etc.	salir-saldré, saldrás, etc.
poder-podré, podrás, etc.	tener-tendré, tendrás, etc.
poner-pondré, pondrás, ec.	venir-vendré, vendrás, etc.
querer-querré, querrás, etc.	haber-habrá (there will be)

B. Write the correct form of the future (irregulars).

1. Yo me haré (will become) rico en el futuro.

   Tú _____

   Ella _____

   Nosotros _____

   Ellos _____

2. Ella no dirá más mentiras.

   Nosotros _____

   Tú _____

   Yo _____

   Los chicos _____

3. Yo podré comprender el subjuntivo.

   Uds. _____

   La señorita _____

   Francisco y yo _____

   Luisa y su hermana _____

4. Tú no pondrás ni crema ni azúcar en el café.

   Nosotros _____

   Los secretarios _____

   Mi tío _____

   Su papá y tú _____

5. Ella vendrá a la escuela en helicóptero en 2025.

   Yo _____

   Tú _____

   Los profesores y yo _____

6. Ellos tendrán mucho dinero después de graduarse.

Nosotros _____

Yo _____

Conchita _____

Pedro y tú _____

7. Yo saldré para España en el verano.

Mercedes _____

Tú _____

Las amigas _____

Ud. y su papá _____

8. Ellos sabrán tocar el piano muy bien el año próximo.

Ella _____

Tú _____

Uds. _____

9. Yo querré dormir poco cuando tendré 80 años.

Tú _____

Ellos _____

Nosotros _____

10. Ellos se pondrán el abrigo en Alaska.

Uds. _____

Nosotras _____

Tú _____

C. Review. Write the future (*el futuro*).

1. estar	tú		Uds.
2. saber	yo		ella
3. cantar	nosotros		él
4. hacer	Luisa		tú
5. llegar	Uds.		yo
6. comer	ella		nosotros
7. poder	él		ellas
8. salir	yo		Uds.
9. venir	nosotros		tú
10. tener	María		ellos

D. Review. Translate.

1. I will buy a new car next month.

_____

2. They will be here next year.

_____

3. She will live in Colombia in three years.

_____

4. He will fix his car and then he'll go to work.

_____

5. You (*fam.*) will not drink if you will drive.

_____

6. We will have a lot of money in six years.

_____

7. They will be able to understand French in a few semesters.

_____

8. The teacher will give an easy quiz.

_____

9. I will not tell white lies.

_____

10. We will get up early and then will go on vacation.

_____

11. There will not be class next week.

_____

12. He will go out with her soon.

_____

13. Will you (*fam.*) come to school next semester?

_____

14. Where will our parents live in five years?

_____

15. I will write a great novel.

_____

37 IMPERFECT SUBJUNCTIVE

The imperfect subjunctive (*el imperfecto de subjuntivo*) is formed by using the third person plural of the preterite as the stem, deleting -ON and by adding the following endings: **a, as, a, amos, an.**

Imperfect Subjunctive

ellos cantar~~on~~	ellos comier~~on~~	ellos escribier~~on~~
yo cantara	yo comiera	yo escribiera
tú cantaras	tú comieras	tú escribieras
Ud. cantara	Ud. comiera	Ud. escribiera
él, ella cantara	él, ella comiera	él, ella escribiera
nosotros cantáramos	nosotros comiéramos	nosotros escribiéramos
Uds. cantaran	Uds. comieran	Uds. escribieran
ellos, ellas cantaran	ellos, ellas comieran	ellos, ellas escribieran

TIP: *Review the preterite of regular and irregular verbs before doing these exercises.*

A. Write the imperfect subjunctive (*el imperfecto de subjuntivo*). The first one is given to you; you should figure out the rest easily. As you do exercises **A** and **B**, note that the trigger for the imperfect subjunctive is either an imperfect (*dudaban* in # 1) or a preterite (*creyeron* in # 2).

1. Dudaban que yo hablara con el presidente.

    "   " tú _____

    "   " Ud. _____

    "   " nosotros _____

    "   " ellos _____

2. No creyeron que Uds. comieran enchiladas en el restaurante japonés.

    " " " yo _____

    " " " ella _____

    " " " Luisa y yo _____

    " " " tú _____

3. Les gustó que nosotros no miráramos ese horrible programa.

    " " " yo no _____

    " " " tú no _____

    " " " ellas no _____

    " " " Ud. no _____

4. No era verdad que ellos estudiaran mucho.

    " " " " ella _____

    " " " tú _____

    " " " " nosotros _____

    " " " " yo _____

5. Era posible que Luis cantara mi canción favorita en la fiesta.

    " " " ellas _____

    " " " tú _____

    " " " Ud. _____

    " " " Pedro y tú _____

6. No creyeron que yo leyera la novela rápidamente.

    " " " Uds._____

    " " " nosotros _____

7. Esperaba que Uds. hicieran toda la tarea.

    " " yo _____

    " " Luis y yo _____

8. Dudaban que tú fueras a México en autostop.

    " " el doctor _____

    " " las chicas _____

9. Luis esperaba que tu papá me diera el dinero.

    " " " ellas me _____

    " " " Uds. me _____

10. No creíamos que ella fuera una estudiante excelente.

    " " " tú _____

    " " " ellos _____

11. Era necesario que nosotros estuviéramos allí.

    " " " tú _____

    " " " Uds. _____

12. Era posible que ella viniera a la fiesta.

    " " " Uds. _____

    " " " nosotros _____

Imperfect Subjunctive

13. Sentíamos que ella no quisiera estudiar en esta universidad.

"   " tú _____

"   " Uds. _____

14. Dudaban que yo pudiera estar allí a las dos de la mañana.

"   " nosotros _____

"   " ellos _____

15. No fue posible que yo supiera toda la verdad.

" " " " tú _____

" " " " nosotros _____

16. No creía que tú tuvieras todo el tiempo.

" " " nosotros _____

" " " Uds. _____

B. Write the imperfect subjunctive (*el imperfecto de subjuntivo*).

1. Era posible que Pedro (comprar) _____ el coche nuevo.

2. Dudaban que yo (estar) _____ en la escuela el sábado.

3. No estaban seguros que Uds. (visitar) _____ cinco países en tres días.

4. Me alegraba que él nos (invitar) _____ a la fiesta.

5. Era posible que tú no (tratar) _____ de resolver el problema.

6. Negaron que ella me (escribir) _____ muchas tarjetas.

7. Sentíamos que sus hijas no (aprender) _____ mucho en la clase.

8. Ojalá que ellos no te (pedir) _____ mucho dinero por ese coche viejo.

9. ¿Era posible que ellos no (ir) _____ a su clase en el día del examen final?

10. Fue una lástima que yo no (hacer) _____ nada interesante.

11. Fue imposible que ellos no (oír) _____ la explosión.

12. Dudaban que María me (decir) _____ todos sus secretos.

Imperfect Subjunctive

13. No era posible que tú (descubrir) _____ toda la verdad.

14. No creían que tú (dormir) _____ trece horas.

15. A mi padre le gustó que mi novia (venir) _____ a nuestra casa a cenar.

16. Esperaban que yo les (traer) _____ la comida en la oficina.

17. Querían que tú (ser) _____ una buena estudiante.

18. Era imposible que nosotros (leer) _____ todos esos libros.

19. Temían que muchos invitados no (estar) _____ en la boda.

20. No creyó que Uds. (poder) _____ venir a clase.

21. Esperaba que yo (tener) _____ el tiempo para ir de compras con ellos.

22. No estaba seguro que ella te (dar) _____ su número de teléfono.

23. Nos alegramos que ellos nos (decir) _____ la verdad.

C. Review. Write the imperfect subjunctive (*el imperfecto de subjuntivo*).

1. mirar	yo	Uds.
2. estudiar	Uds.	tú
3. vivir	tú	nosotros
4. escribir	nosotros	él
5. hacer	él	ellos
6. dar	ellos	yo
7. traer	tú	ellas
8. poder	Uds.	tú
9. ir	ella	nosotros
10. ser	yo	Uds.

D. Review. Translate.

1. They didn't believe I visited six countries in four days.

_____

2. It was not true that we ate in that restaurant.

_____

3. It was possible that he would buy a new car.

_____

4. I didn't think that the doctor would arrive on time.

_____

5. We were glad that you (*pl.*) visited Mexico and Guatemala.

_____

6. They doubted that he would do many favors for me.

_____

7. It was a pity that they would ask me for money.

_____

8. We hoped they would tell him the story.

_____

9. It was probable that her father would return from Europe with many
gifts.

_____

10. It was incredible that her sons would learn how to play the piano and
the guitar in three months.

_____

11. I hoped that they would solve their difficult problem.

_____

12. It was not possible that she would fall and would not break her legs.

_____

13. It was important for him to be able to be there.

_____

14. They did not think we did all the homework in ten minutes.

_____

15. She wanted us to bring the beer to the party.

_____

16. We hoped that they would come to class on time.

_____

17. He was glad that they were nice people.

_____

18. She doubted that we would go to Spain for only two days.

_____

19. The parents feared that the children would want to eat pizza again.

_____

20. It was impossible for you (*form.*) to know all the new vocabulary.

_____

21. We did not think he would put salt in the pie.

_____

22. We hoped that the baby would sleep for fifteen hours.

_____

23. I doubted that there would be an exam today.

_____

24. She was sorry that they were not present at her wedding.

_____

TIPS. *As you noticed in the exercises, the imperfect subjunctive can translate into English with a conditional, an infinitive, or a past tense.*
• *You should have also noticed that the imperfect subjunctive is used when the main clause contains a "trigger" in the imperfect or preterite.*

Imperfect Subjunctive

38 CONDITIONAL

The conditional tense (*el condicional*) is formed by using the infinitive of the verb as the stem and adding the following endings: **ía, ías, ía, íamos, ían.**

Note that the endings for the conditional are identical to those of the imperfect indicative of the second and third conjugation verbs. Thus, the difference in forms between the conditional and the imperfect of these verbs is the stem:

conditional: *comería, viviría, escribiría*
imperfect: *comía, vivía, escribía*

The only irregularities in the conditional appear in the stem. The endings are always the same for all three conjugations. The irregular stems for the conditional are exactly the same as those for the future.

The conditional in English uses the auxiliary "would" and the verb. The "condition" is often expressed but sometimes it is implied:

*I **would go** with you to Iran, but I am very busy.*
*Pedro said he **would be** here this evening.*

Conditional

hablar	comer	escribir
yo hablaría	yo comería	yo escribiría
ú hablarías	tú comerías	tú escribirías
Ud. hablaría	Ud. comería	Ud. escribiría
él, ella hablaría	él, ella comería	él, ella escribiría
nosotros hablaríamos	nosotros comeríamos	nosotros escribiríamos
Uds. hablarían	Uds. comerían	Uds. escribirían
ellos, ellas hablarían	ellos, ellas comerían	ellos, ellas escribirían

A. Write the conditional (*el condicional*) (regular verbs).

1. Yo cantaría en francés, pero prefiero cantar en español.

Ud. _____

Tú _____

Ellas _____

Conditional

2. Tú mirarías la tele, pero tienes que hacer la tarea.

Uds. _____

Él _____

Nosotros _____

3. Los chicos estudiarían todo el capítulo, pero están muy cansados.

María _____

Tú _____

El doctor y yo _____

4. Yo hablaría con Ud., pero prefiero hablar con los otros chicos.

Nosotras _____

La enfermera _____

Uds. _____

5. Ella arreglaría tu coche, pero tú no quieres pagar bastante.

Yo _____

Tú _____

Los profesores y yo _____

6. Ellos buscarían a sus amigos, pero no pueden hacerlo sin coche.

Nosotros _____

Yo _____

Conchita _____

7. Yo estaría en casa ahora, pero necesito trabajar aquí.

Mercedes _____

Tú _____

Ud. y su papá _____

8. Ellos tocarían el piano muy bien, pero no quieren practicar cuatro
horas al día.

Ella _____

Tú _____

Uds. _____

9. Yo me acostaría temprano, pero me gusta mirar las películas en la
noche.

Tú _____

Ellos _____

Nosotros _____

10. Ellos se levantarían tarde, pero necesitan estar en la oficina a las ocho
en punto.

Nosotras _____

Tú _____

Sus hermanos _____

11. Ellas vivirían en Santa Bárbara, pero la ciudad es muy cara.

Yo _____

Nosotros _____

La criada _____

12. Ellas leerían poco, pero tienen que completar una novela cada semana
en la clase de literatura.

Yo _____

Carlos y yo _____

Tú _____

13. Ella bebería mucho vino en Inglaterra, pero el vino inglés es malo y
caro.

Nosotros _____

Mi familia _____

Tus amigos _____

14. Tú no insistirías en hablar inglés, pero a veces no comprendes nada
porque la profesora habla muy rápido.

El secretario _____

Tú _____

Las señoras _____

15. Ella no se dormiría en clase, pero está muy cansada.

Ellos _____

Nosotras _____

El chico rubio _____

B. Write the conditional (*el condicional*) (irregulars).

1. Yo me haría rico en poco tiempo.

Tú _____

Nosotros _____

Ellos _____

2. Ella no diría mentiritas, pero no quiere ofender a nadie.

Nosotros _____

Los chicos _____

3. Yo podría comprender el subjuntivo, pero hay muchos verbos
irregulares.

    Francisco y yo _____

    Luisa y su hermana _____

4. Tú te pondrías la chaqueta, pero no hace mucho frío.

    Nosotros _____

    Los secretarios _____

5. Ella vendría a la escuela a las ocho, pero no tiene clase hasta las diez.

    Tú _____

    Los profesores y yo _____

6. Ellos tendrían mucho dinero, pero les gusta usar su tarjeta de crédito
con frecuencia.

    Nosotros _____

    Yo _____

7. Yo saldría para París en seguida, pero tengo que trabajar.

    Tú _____

    Las amigas _____

8. Ellos sabrían tocar el saxofón muy bien, pero no les gusta practicar
    mucho.

    Tú _____

    La enfermera _____

9. Yo querría descansar, pero tengo que aprender el vocabulario.

    Ellos _____

    Nosotros _____

C. Review. Write the conditional (*el condicional*).

1. estar	tú		ellas
2. tocar	yo		nosotros
3. insistir	ella		Uds.
4. dormirse	nosotros		él
5. hacer	Uds.		La chica
6. poner	él		tú
7. salir	la chica		ellas
8. decir	tú		yo
9. ir	ella		nosotros
10. tener	yo		ellos

D. Review. Translate.

1. We would speak Spanish, but he does not understand the language.

_____

2. The student would read the entire novel for tomorrow, but it is too
   long.

_____

3. They would live in San Francisco, but it's too expensive.

_____

4. I would drink wine, but I would fall asleep immediately.

_____

5. You (*form.*) would have a lot of money, but you like to use your credit
   card too much.

_____

6. She would tell us everything, but she does not know it.

_____

7. He would put his jacket on, but it's not cold.

_____

8. You (*fam.*) would become rich, but you do not like to work twenty
   hours a day.

_____

9. I would leave the house at six, but I do not get up until eight.

_____

10. They would give you (*pl.*) all their money, but it would not be enough to
pay all your bills.

_____

_____

11. She would come to Europe, but she needs to finish school first.

_____

12. We would be home now, but we have to see our French instructor at
    1:00.

_____

13. Would you (*fam.*) go to Las Vegas by train?

_____

14. I would say something, but I am afraid to speak in front of a large group.

_____

15. She would make me a cake, but she does not have all the ingredients.

_____

39 REVIEW OF VERBS

A. Review of verbs. Conjugation. Write the correct form of each verb.

INDICATIVE (*indicativo*)	mirar-yo
1. present (*presente*)	
2. imperfect (*imperfecto*)	
3. preterite (*pretérito*)	
4. future (*futuro*)	
5. conditional (*condicional*)	
6. present perfect (*presente perfecto*)	
SUBJUNCTIVE (*subjuntivo*)	
7. present (*presente*)	
8. present perfect (*presente perfecto*)	
9. imperfect (*imperfecto*)	
COMMAND (*mandato*)	mirar
10. Ud.	
11. Uds.	
12. tú (*negative*)	
13. tú (*affirmative*)	

Review of Verbs

B. Review of verbs. Conjugation. Write the correct form of the verbs.

INDICATIVE	leer-tú
1. present	
2. imperfect	
3. preterite	
4. future	
5. conditional	
6. present perfect	
SUBJUNCTIVE	
7. present	
8. present perfect	
9. imperfect	
COMMAND	leer
10. Ud.	
11. Uds.	
12. tú (*negative*)	
13. tú (*affirmative*)	

C. Review of verbs. Conjugation. Write the correct form of the verbs.

INDICATIVE	decir-Ud.
1. present	
2. imperfect	
3. preterite	
4. future	
5. conditional	
6. present perfect	
SUBJUNCTIVE	
7. present	
8. present perfect	
9. imperfect	
COMMAND	decir
10. Ud.	
11. Uds.	
12. tú (*negative*)	
13. tú (*affirmative*)	

D. Review of verbs. Conjugation. Write the correct form of the verbs.

INDICATIVE	empezar-nosotros
1. present	
2. imperfect	
3. preterite	
4. future	
5. conditional	
6. present perfect	
SUBJUNCTIVE	
7. present	
8. present perfect	
9. imperfect	
COMMAND	empezar
10. Ud.	
11. Uds.	
12. tú (*negative*)	
13. tú (*affirmative*)	

E. Review of verbs. Conjugation. Write the correct form of the verbs.

INDICATIVE	volver-ellos
1. present	
2. imperfect	
3. preterite	
4. future	
5. conditional	
6. present perfect	
SUBJUNCTIVE	
7. present	
8. present perfect	
9. imperfect	
COMMAND	volver
10. Ud.	
11. Uds.	
12. tú (*negative*)	
13. tú (*affirmative*)	

F. Translate.

1. I speak _____
2. I used to speak _____
3. I was speaking _____
4. I spoke yesterday _____
5. I will speak _____
6. I would speak _____
7. I have spoken _____
8. They doubt I speak _____
9. They doubt I spoke/have spoken _____
10. They doubted I would speak _____
11. Speak! (Ud.) _____
12. Speak! (Uds.) _____
13. Don't speak! (tú) _____
14. Speak! (tú) _____

G. Translate.

1. You (fam.) eat _____
2. You used to eat _____
3. You were eating _____
4. You ate yesterday _____
5. You will eat _____
6. You would eat _____
7. You have eaten _____
8. They doubt that you eat _____
9. They doubt you ate/have eaten _____
10. They doubted you would eat _____
11. Eat! (Ud.) _____
12. Eat! (Uds.) _____
13. Don't eat! (tú) _____
14. Eat! (tú) _____

H. Translate.

1. She writes _____
2. She used to write _____
3. She was writing _____
4. She wrote yesterday _____
5. She will write _____

6. She would write _____

7. She has written _____

8. They doubt that she writes _____

9. They doubt that she wrote/has written _____

10. They doubted that she would write _____

11. Write! (Ud.) _____

12. Write! (Uds.) _____

13. Don't write! (tú) _____

14. Write! (tú) _____

I. Translate (use *saber*)

1. We know _____

2. We used to know _____

3. We knew _____

4. We found out _____

5. We will know _____

6. We would know _____

7. We have known _____

8. They doubt that we know _____

9. They doubt we have known/knew _____

10. They doubted we would know _____

11. Know! (Ud.) _____

12. Know! (Uds.) _____

13. Know! (tú) _____

J. Translate

1. They go _____

2. They used to go _____

3. They were going _____

4. They went yesterday _____

5. They will go _____

6. They would go _____

7. They have gone _____

8. We doubt that they go _____

9. We doubt that they went/have gone _____

10. We doubted that they would go _____

11. Go! (Ud.) _____

12. Go! (Uds.) _____

Review of Verbs

13. Don't go! (tú) _____

14. Go! (tú) _____

40 ANSWER KEY

1. Singular Nouns and Articles
A. 1.una 2.una 3.un 4.una 5.un 6.un 7.una 8.un 9.un 10.una
B. 1.un 2.una 3.una 4.un 5.una 6.una 7.un 8.una 9.una 10.una
C. 1.un 2.una 3.un 4.una 5.un 6.una 7.un 8.un 9.un 10.un 11.una 12.una 13.un 14.una 15.un 16.una
D. 1.la 2.el 3.el 4.la 5.el 6.la 7.el 8.el 9.el 10.el 11.la 12.la 13.la 14.el 15.el 16.el
E. 1.un estudiante 2.el saxofón 3.un lápiz 4.la casa 5.una noche 6.un día 7.una oficina 8.el secretario 9.el problema 10.una mujer 11.un hombre 12.la tarde 13.la situación 14.una ciudad 15.un doctor 16.la amiga 17.la artista 18.un libro 19.un elefante 20.el dentista

2. Plural Nouns and Articles
A. 1.los libros 2.las casas 3.las personas 4.los problemas 5.los profesores 6.unas clientes 7.unas oficinas 8.unos amigos 9.unas socialistas 10.unos días
B. 1.una amiga 2.un laboratorio 3.un hombre 4.una tarde 5.un dentista 6.la doctora 7.el dependiente 8.la parte 9.el día 10.la situación 11.el papel 12.el mapa
C. 1.unos 2.unas 3.unos 4.unas 5.unos 6.unas 7.unos 8.unos 9.unos 10.unos 11.unas 12.unas 13.unos 14.unas 15.unos 16.unas
D. 1.las 2.los 3.los 4.las 5.los 6.las 7.los 8.los 9.los 10.los 11.las 12.las 13.las 14.los 15.los 16.los
E. 1.las dentistas 2.unos elefantes 3.unos libros 4.las artistas 5.unas amigas 6.unos doctores 7.unas ciudades 8.las situaciones 9.las tardes 10.unos hombres 11.unas mujeres 12.los problemas 13.los secretarios 14.unas oficinas 15.unos días 16.las noches 17.unas casas 18.unos lápices 19.los saxofones 20.unos estudiantes

3. Subject Pronouns
A. 1.he 2.I 3.we 4.they (masc.) 5.you (form.) 6.we (fem.) 7.they (fem.) 8.you (fam.) 9.you (pl.) 10.she.
B. 1.ch 2.h 3.e 4.f 5.i 6.b 7.g 8.a 9.d 10.c.
C. 1.tú 2.Ud 3.Uds. 4.tú 5.Uds. 6.Uds. 7.Ud. 8.tú
D. 1.ella 2.ellos 3.ellas 4.él 5.nosotros 6.ellos (ellas) 7.yo 8.nosotros
E. 1.ellos 2.yo 3.ella 4.Ud. 5.él 6.tú 7.nosotros 8.ellas 9.Uds. 10.nosotras
F. 1.Ud. 2.él 3.Uds. 4.nosotros 5.ellas 6.yo 7.ella 8.tú 9.nosotras 10.ellos

4. Present Tense of -AR Verbs
A. 1.yo 2.tú 3.Ud., él, ella 4.nosotros 5.Uds., ellos, ellas 6.yo 7.nosotros 8.tú 9.Ud., él, ella 10.nosotros 11.Uds., ellos, ellas 12.yo 13.tú 14.Ud., él, ella 15. Uds., ellos, ellas 16.nosotros
B. 1.o 2.an 3.amos 4.an 5.as 6.a 7.an 8.amos.

C. 1.canto 2.baila 3.trabajan 4.pagas 5. enseñan 6.estudia 7.compramos 8.toma

D. 1.you speak 2. he speaks 3.she speaks 4.you study 5.he pronounces 6.she pronounces 7.he practices 8.you practice 9.she buys 10.he works

E. 1.ella-she studies 2.ella-she practices 3.ella-she pronounces 4.ella-she buys 5.él-he dances 6.él-he desires 7.él-he pays 8. él-he returns 9. ella-she needs 10. él-he teaches

F. 1.you (pl.) speak 2.they (fem.) speak 3.they (masc.) speak 4.you (pl.) practice 5.they (fem.) study 6.you (pl.) pronounce 7.they (masc.) sing 8. you (pl.) look for 9.they (masc.) return 10.they (masc.) take, drink

G. 1.ellas-they speak 2.ellas-they dance 3.ellas-they work 4.ellas-they take, drink 5.ellas-they return 6.ellas-they study 7.ellos-they sing 8. ellos-they buy 9.ellos-they need 10.ellos-they pay.

H. 1.estudiamos 2.practicamos 3. pronunciamos 4.bailamos 5. trabajamos 6. buscamos 7. pagamos 8. necesitamos 9. enseñamos 10. tomamos

I. 1.toman 2.practican 3.cantan 4.necesitan 5.hablan 6.desean 7. compran 8. bailan 9. trabajan 10. pagan.

J. 1.yo-I study 2.tú-you work 3.Ud., él, ella-you, s/he desire/s 4.nosotros-we dance 5. Uds., ellos, ellas-you (pl.), they look for 6.yo-I teach 7. tú-you speak 8. Ud., él, ella-you, s/he need/s 9.nosotros-we pay 10. Uds., ellos, ellas-you (pl.),they practice 11.yo-I return 12.tú-you take, drink, 13.Ud., él, ella-you, s/he work/s 14.Uds., ellos, ellas-you (pl.), they dance 15.nosotros-we look for.

K. 1.habla 2.deseamos 3.necesitan 4.pago 5.trabajan 6.tomamos 7.enseñas 8.bailan 9.busca 10.practican

L. 1.El profesor (la profesora) habla francés 2. Los estudiantes estudian. 3. Frank y yo practicamos. 4.¿Tú trabajas? 5.Yo necesito pagar. 6.Julio Iglesias no canta muy bien. 7.Nosotros bailamos en la fiesta. 8.Ellas regresan a casa. 9.Uds. toman café en la mañana. 10.Pedro enseña en la tarde. 11.Yo no deseo regresar a la universidad. 12.Nosotros buscamos el laboratorio.

5. Present Tense of *Estar*

A. 1.yo 2.nosotros 3.tú 4.Uds. 5.ellas 6.ellos 7.Ud. 8.él

B. 1.estamos 2.están 3.están 4.está 5.están 6.está 7.estás 8.está

C. 1.está 2.están 3.está 4.estamos 5.está 6.está 7.está 8.está 9.estamos 10.está 11.están 12.está 13.estoy 14.está 15. está

D. 1.El profesor Hernández está en la oficina. 2. Nosotros no estamos bien. 3.El taco está delicioso. 4.¿Dónde estás tú a las diez de la mañana? 5.¿Está claro? 6.Ellos están nerviosos porque tienen un examen de matemáticas. 7.Él no está ocupado ahora. 8.Guadalajara está en México. 9.Yo estoy sentado al lado de María. 10.La minifalda no está de moda. 11.Luisa no está de acuerdo con el profesor de español. 12.¿La biblioteca está abierta o cerrada los sábados? 13.Mi abuelo está cansado en la tarde. 14.Yo estoy aburrido. 15.¿Cómo estás tú?

6. Present Tense of *Ser*

A. 1.nosotros 2.yo 3.tú 4.Uds. 5.tú 6.ellos 7.Ud. 8.él

B. 1.es 2.eres 3.es 4.son 5.es 6.son 7.son 8.somos

C. 1.es 2.son 3.son 4.somos 5.son 6.es 7.es 8.es 9.es 10.es 11.es 12.es 13.es 14.son 15.son

D. 1.Yo soy de Barcelona. 2.Los estudiantes son responsables. 3.El carro no es viejo. 4.La cerveza es para Pancho. 5.¿Qué es esto? 6.Son las diez de la noche. 7.La mesa es de madera. 8. Luisa es doctora. 9.No es práctico mirar la televisión doce horas al día. 10¿De dónde es Ud.? 11.Ellos son buenos amigos. 12.Mis padres no son ricos. 13.Es el coche de Linda. 14.Los Angeles no es la capital de California. 15.Mi hermana quiere ser sicóloga.

7. Descriptive Adjectives

A. 1.los chicos altos 2.las mujeres ricas 3.los pacientes sentimentales 4.las doctoras inteligentes 5.los coches verdes 6.las casas viejas 7.los jóvenes franceses 8.las ciudades holandesas 9.los doctores trabajadores 10.las señoritas japonesas 11.los restaurantes ingleses 12.los clientes irlandeses
B. 1. alta, danesa, formal, mexicana, fiel 2.morenos, casados, jóvenes 3.grande, interesante, fascinante, gris, azul 4.importante, excelente, terrible 5.nuevo, caro, verde 6.largas, formales, democráticas
C. 1.un hombre alto 2.una doctora rica 3.un paciente amable 4.el alumno pobre 5.la chica inteligente 6.una clase grande 7.la señorita alemana 8.la lección larga 9.el lápiz rojo 10.un secretario impaciente 11.la gran ciudad 12.el gran presidente 13. una enchilada deliciosa 14.el buen amigo 15.el edificio bueno 16.la silla cómoda 17.un diccionario completo 18.un pobre turista 19.la hermosa ciudad de París 20.la pequeña ciudad de Sisquoc 21.el amigo viejo 22.la gran parte 23.una bicicleta nueva 24.su guapo esposo
D 1.los libros viejos 2.las señoras ricas 3.los doctores ingleses 4.las clientes holandesas 5.las lecciones largas 6.los chicos trabajadores
E. THE CORRECT NUMBERS ARE: 1,4, 6,7,10
F. 1.una clase interesante 2.los verdes pinos 3.el mal doctor 4.una silla cómoda 5.un elefante pequeño 6.un gran hombre 7.un viejo amigo 8.su guapo esposo

8. Present Tense of -*ER* and -*IR* Verbs

A. 1.yo 2.tú 3.Ud., él, ella 4.nosotros 5.Uds, ellos, ellas 6.yo 7.nosotros 8.tú 9.Ud., él, ella 10.nosotros
B. 1.o 2.en 3.emos 4.en 5.es 6.e 7.en 8.imos 9.en 10.o
C. 1.vendo 2.abre 3.aprenden 4.bebes 5.comprenden 6.asiste 7.recibimos 8.insiste 9.creo 10.vive 11.deben 12.comemos 13.venden 14.lees 15.debemos 16.cree
D. 1.yo-I open 2.tú-you (fam.) attend 3.Ud.,él, ella-you (form.) s/he write/s 4.nosotros-we receive 5.Uds., ellos, ellas-you (pl.), they live 6.yo-I sell 7.tú-you (fam.) drink 8.Ud., él, ella-you (form.), s/he eat/s 9. nosotros-we understand 10. Uds., ellos, ellas-you (pl.), they believe 11. yo-I must 12.tú-you (fam.) read 13. Ud.,él, ella-you (form.), s/he sell/s 14. nosotros-we open 15.Uds., ellos, ellas-you (pl.), they attend
E. 1.vive 2.aprendemos 3.abren 4.bebo 5.venden 6.escribimos 7.insistes 8.leen 9.recibo 10.creen
F. 1.El profesor (la profesora) come mucho. 2.Los estudiantes abren el libro. 3.Frank y yo leemos. 4.¿Tú escribes? 5.Yo debo pagar. 6.Los niños reciben muchos regalos. 7.Nosotros no bebemos mucho en las fiestas. 8.Ellas aprenden

mucho. 9.Uds. no venden sus libros de español. 10.Pedro vive en Santa Bárbara. 11.Mi hija cree en Santa Claus. 12.Yo no asisto a clases en la noche. 13.¿El presidente comprende mis problemas? 14.Algunos estudiantes insisten en hablar inglés en la clase de francés.

9. Possessive Adjectives

A. 1.mi 2.nuestra 3.sus 4.tus 5.nuestros
B. 1.sus gatos 2.nuestras casas 3.tus mesas 4.nuestros libros 5.sus doctoras 6.mis perros
C. 1.mi/mis 2.su/sus 3.nuestro/nuestros 4.tus/tu 5.su/sus 6.su
D. 1.mis amigos 2.su camisa 3.su padre 4. sus padres 5.tu carro 6.nuestro abuelo 7.sus clases 8.sus gatos 9.nuestro presidente 10.tus ideas 11.su novio 12.sus zapatos 13.mi casa 14.su radio 15.sus hermanas 16.su sombrero

10. Present Tense of *tener, venir, preferir, querer, poder*

A. 1.yo-I come 2.tú-you (fam.) can 3.Ud., él, ella-you (form.), s/he prefer/s 4.nosotros-we come 5.Uds., ellos, ellas-you (pl.), they have 6.yo-I can 7.tú-you want 8.Ud., él, ella-you (form.), s/he come/s 9.nosotros-we prefer 10.yo-I have
B. 1.puedes 2.quieren 3.puedo 4.vienen 5.tiene 6.podemos 7.quieren 8.vengo 9.tienen 10.preferimos
C. 1.Yo no tengo mucho dinero. 2.Nosotros queremos aprender francés. 3.Los estudiantes vienen a la escuela a tiempo. 4.Bill Clinton prefiere comer en McDonald's. 5. Mi padre y yo podemos tocar el piano. 6.El doctor no puede venir a su casa. 7.Julio Iglesias quiere cantar en inglés. 8.¿Puedes comer once enchiladas? 9.Donald Trump y Marla Maples prefieren vivir en Nueva York. 10.Imelda Marcos tiene muchos zapatos.

11. *Ir*; *Ir + A +* Infinitive

A. 1.tú 2.yo 3.nosotros 4.Uds. 5.ellas 6.ellos 7. Ud. 8. él 9.ella
B. 1. van 2.vamos 3.va 4.vas 5.voy 6.ir 7.va 8. va
C. 1.vas a comer 2.vamos a practicar 3.van a estudiar 4.vamos a buscar 5.va a recibir 6.voy a escribir 7.va a comprar 8.van a bailar
D. 1.Yo no voy a la escuela los domingos. 2.Nosotros vamos a España. 3.Mi papá va al trabajo todos los días. 4. ¿Adónde vas tú? 5.Él va a practicar mañana. 6.Ellos no quieren ir al laboratorio a las siete de la mañana. 7.Ella va a escribir muchas cartas este fin de semana. 8.Mercedes y yo vamos a tomar una clase de matemáticas.

12. Present Tense of *hacer, oír, poner, salir, traer*, and *ver*

A. 1.yo/I put, place 2.tú/You make, do 3.Ud., él, ella/You go out, leave; s/he goes out, leaves 4.nosotros/We put, place 5.Uds., ellos, ellas/You/they go out, leave 6.Uds., ellos, ellas/You/they make, do 7.yo/I make, do 8.tú/You go out, leave
B. 1.hago 2.sale 3.ponemos 4.hace 5.hacen 6.pones 7.salimos 8.hace

C. 1.yo/I hear 2.tú/You bring 3.Ud., él, ella/You see; s/he sees 4.nosotros/We hear 5.Uds.,ellos, ellas/You/they bring 6.tú/You see 7.yo/I bring 8.Uds., ellos, ellas/You/they hear

D. 1.oigo 2.vemos 3.traes 4.ve. 5.oyen 6.traen

E. 1.¿Qué haces tú los viernes por la noche?. 2.¿A qué hora sale de casa su hermano en la mañana? 3.Nosotros no traemos vino a clase. 4.Yo veo muy bien. Yo no necesito lentes. 5.Luis pone el radio en la tarde. 6.Hace frío ahora. 7.Mi abuelo no oye muy bien. 8.A veces nosotros salimos tarde de la clase de español porque la profesora habla demasiado. 9.Cuando los alumnos no entienden algo ellos hacen preguntas. 10.¿Traen Uds. plumas o lápices para sus exámenes? 11.¿Tu papá pone crema en su café? 12.Yo no puedo oír muy bien ahora.

13. Present Tense of Stem-Changing Verbs

A. 1.cierro 2.empieza 3.entiendes 4.pensamos 5.pierden 6.cerramos 7.empiezan 8.entienden 9. pierde 10.piensa

B. 1.vuelves 2.almuerza 3.dormimos 4.juegan 5.vuelvo 6.duermen 7.almuerzan 8.juega

C. 1.repites 2.pide 3.seguimos 4.sirven 5.pido 6.siguen 7.repiten 8.servimos

D. 1. Nosotros almorzamos a la una. 2.Unos estudiantes piensan ir a Europa en el futuro. 3.La profesora (el profesor) de español empieza a perder su paciencia. 4.Pedro siempre pide tacos y enchiladas. 5.Yo nunca sirvo vino en mis fiestas. 6.¿Cuándo vuelve Ud. a casa? 7.¿Entiendes tú la lección? 8.Mi esposa siempre pierde dinero cuando juega a la lotería. 9.Los estudiantes empiezan a entender español. 10.Mi elefante duerme diez horas al día. 11.Los alumnos repiten las nuevas palabras. 12.Las chicas siguen a los chicos.

14. Reflexive Verbs

A. 1.te 2.nos 3.me 4.se 5.se 6.nos 7.se 8.se 9.me 10.nos

B. 1.me 2.se 3.te 4.se 5.nos 6.se 7.se 8.me 9.me 10.te 11.te 12.nos 13.nos 14.te 15.te

C. 1. Linda se levanta temprano. 2.Nosotros no nos afeitamos todos los días. 3.Ellos se duermen en clase. 4.Él se ducha una o dos veces al día. 5.Yo nunca me maquillo en clase. 6.Muchos estudiantes se sientan enfrente. 7.Pancho prefiere sentarse al lado de María. 8. Mercedes y tú se quedan aquí hasta las cinco de la tarde. 9. Nosotros nos vestimos de prisa. 10.Yo me baño todos los días. 11.Carlos se divierte en mis fiestas. 12.¿Te vas a acostar pronto?/¿Vas a acostarte pronto? 13.A veces yo no me puedo dormir muy rápido/ A veces yo no puedo dormirme muy rápido. 14.Mi hijo no se quiere despertar temprano los domingos/Mi hijo no quiere despertarse temprano los domingos. 15.Antonio se sienta al lado de Luisa.

15. Demonstrative Adjectives

A. 1.estas mesas 2.estos muchachos 3.aquellas señoras 4.esos vestidos 5.aquellos almacenes 6.estas estudiantes 7.esas casas 8.aquellas situaciones 9.esos relojes 10.aquellas chaquetas

B. 1.b 2.a 3.b 4.a 5.b 6.b

C. 1.ese vestido 2.aquellos chicos 3.este carro y ése 4.Eso es terrible 5.esa situación 6.estas historias 7.aquella casa 8.Eso es magnífico. 9.estos relojes 10.esta camisa 11.esos exámenes 12.esa mochila

16. Present Progressive

A. 1.bailando 2.mirando 3.comiendo 4.leyendo 5.viviendo 6.trayendo 7.sirviendo 8.perdiendo 9.haciendo 10.aprendiendo

B. 1.está fumando 2.estamos jugando 3.estás haciendo 4.están llegando 5.me estoy levantando/estoy levantándome 6.están trabajando 7.está saliendo 8.estamos viviendo 9.están trayendo 10.estás sirviendo 11.estoy recibiendo 12.se está vistiendo/está vistiéndose 13.está vendiendo 14.estamos pidiendo 15.estoy oyendo

C. 1.Generalmente yo como en casa, pero ahora yo estoy comiendo en un restaurante. 2.Generalmente ellos estudian en la biblioteca, pero ahora ellos están estudiando en su carro. 3.Pedro juega al fútbol los viernes, pero ahora está jugando al tenis. 4.Generalmente nosotros miramos la televisión en la noche, pero ahora estamos leyendo. 5.Isabel baila los sábados por la noche, pero ahora ella está haciendo su tarea. 6.¿Estás fumando tú ahora mismo? 7.Ellos se están levantando ahora mismo/Ellos están levantándose ahora mismo. 8.Yo no estoy pidiendo pizza ahora, pero yo voy a pedir pizza más tarde. 9.¿Qué está Ud. haciendo ahora mismo? 10.¿Los estudiantes están pensando en inglés o en español ahora mismo? 11.Nosotros no nos estamos duchando ahora mismo/Nosotros no estamos duchándonos ahora mismo. 12.Ella no está escuchando la radio ahora mismo.

17. *Ser* Vs. *Estar*

A. 1.está 2.son 3.son 4.están 5.es/está 6.está 7.estoy 8.es 9.estás 10.es/están 11.están 12.son 13.es 14.son 15.está 16.son 17.es 18.es 19.estamos 20.es/está 21.es 22.está 23.es 24.es/está 25.es/están 26.es/es/está 27.está/está 28.es/es 29.es 30.ser/estar

B. 1.es 2.está 3.está 4.estoy 5.es 6.está 7.es 8.están 9.es 10.Está

C. 1.El taco está muy bueno. 2.¿Dónde estás a las tres de la mañana? 3.Guanajuato está en México. 4.Mi padre no está contento cuando yo manejo rápido. 5.José Carreras es de España. 6.Esta cerveza es para Francisco porque él mira muchos partidos de fútbol norteamericano. 7.Los estudiantes son muy pobres, pero están contentos de estar en la escuela. 8.El profesor de francés es muy aburrido. 9.¡Qué guapo estás hoy! 10.Somos alemanes. 11.Ella no está de acuerdo con Ud. 12.¿Estás listo? 13.La silla es de metal. 14.Mis abuelos están listos para salir. 15.Yo quiero ser profesor de matemáticas. 16.¿Es necesario ir a clase los viernes? 17.Su camisa es verde. 18.¿Está claro? 19.Son las nueve de la mañana. 20.¿Están Uds. ocupados esta noche?

18. Comparisons

A. 1.más 2.menos 3.más 4.menos 5.más 6.más 7.más 8.más

B. 1.mayor 2.mejor 3.menor 4.peores 5.mejores 6.peor

C. 1.tanta 2.tantas 3.tantos 4.tanto 5.tantas 6.tantos

D. 1.tan 2.tanto 3.tan 4.tan 5.tanto 6.tanto

E. 1.tantos 2.tan 3.tan 4.tantas 5.tantas 6.tanto 7.tan 8.tantos 9.tan 10.tanto
F. 1.tan 2.tanto 3.menos 4.mayores 5.más 6.tan 7.más 8.menor 9.tantas 10.tanto
G. 1.Ella habla tan despacio como yo. 2.Nosotros no bebemos (tomamos) tanto café como el profesor de francés. 3.Los coches pequeños son más baratos que los grandes. 4.¿Los plomeros ganan tanto como los doctores? 5.Yo no escribo tan rápido como mi hermano. 6.Los exámenes de matemáticas son más difíciles que los exámenes de español. 7.¿Eres tú mayor o menor que tu hermana? 8.Las clases a las siete de la mañana son peores que las clases a las nueve de la mañana. 9.Nosotros comemos tantas enchiladas como Uds. 10.Ellos no tienen menos amigos que yo. 11.Yo compro tantos zapatos como tú. 12.Nosotros somos tan ricos como nuestras hermanas.

19. *Saber & Conocer*

A. 1-S 2-C 3-S 4-C 5-S 6-S 7-C 8-S 9-S 10-S
B. 1.conoce/sabe 2.sabe/sabe 3.conocemos/sabemos 4.saben 5.sabemos 6.conozco/sé 7.sabemos 8.conocen
C. 1.(Yo) conozco a Luis muy bien, pero no sé dónde vive. 2.(Ella) quiere conocer a mis amigos mexicanos. 3.Sabemos hacer excelentes enchiladas. 4.¿Conoce Ud. muchos restaurantes en California? 5.Conocen Francia, pero no saben hablar francés. 6.Pancho conoce a Mercedes, pero no sabe dónde ella estudia el italiano. 7.El secretario (la secretaria) sabe escribir a máquina rápidamente. 8.Los alumnos conocen a su profesora, pero no saben su número de teléfono. 9.Algunos doctores no conocen a sus pacientes muy bien. 10.Nosotros sabemos que el presidente está en Washington ahora.

20. Direct Object Pronouns

A. 1.it 2.them 3.them 4.them 5.him 6.them
B. 1.Ellos la compran. 2.Pedro los lee. 3.Tú lo necesitas. 4.Nosotros las conocemos. 5.Los alumnos las quieren. 6.Uds. los esperan. 7.Ellas los invitan. 8.Los doctores lo llaman.
C. 1.lo 2.las 3.la 4.nos 5.te 6.los
D. 1.lo 2.me 3.lo 4.la 5.las 6.nos
E. 1.Sí, yo la invito. 2.Sí, yo los llamo. 3.Sí, yo los conozco. 4.Sí, yo las compro. 5.Sí, yo las sé. 6.No, yo no lo traigo a la clase. 7.Sí, yo los espero. 8.Sí, yo los ayudo.
F. 1. Sí, yo lo-la llamo. 2.Sí, yo lo-la conozco. 3.Sí, yo lo-la miro. 4.Sí, yo lo-la busco. 5.Sí, yo lo-la espero.
G. 1.Sí, yo te invito. 2.Sí, yo te llamo. 3.Sí, yo te veo. 4.Sí, yo te espero. 5.Sí, yo te busco.
H. 1.Sí, yo los busco. 2.Sí, yo los miro. 3.Sí, yo los veo. 4.Sí, yo los espero. 5.Sí, yo los invito.
I. 1.Sí, yo voy a comerlas/Yo las voy a comer. 2.Sí, yo voy a leerlos/Yo los voy a leer. 3.Sí, yo quiero invitarlo/Yo lo quiero invitar. 4.Sí, yo deseo llamarlo-la/Yo lo-la deseo llamar. 5.Sí, yo necesito verlos-las/Yo los-las necesito ver. 6.Sí, yo puedo ayudarlos/Yo los puedo ayudar.

J. 1.Sí, yo las compro. 2.Sí, yo los miro. 3.Sí, nosotros los estudiamos. 4.Sí, yo lo-la conozco. 5.Sí, ellos me llaman por teléfono. 6.Sí, yo lo veo. 7.Sí, ellos los esperan. 8.Sí, nosotros las invitamos. 9.Sí, yo te busco. 10.Sí, ellos los leen. 11.Sí, yo las toco. 12.Sí, Uds. me buscan. 13.Sí, yo deseo invitarlos/los deseo invitar. 14.Sí, nosotros podemos llamarte (lo-la)/Nosotros te (lo-la) podemos llamar. 15.Sí, yo voy a escribirlos/los voy a escribir.

K. 1. Yo hago el café y ellos lo beben. 2.Ella no nos ve y nosotros no la vemos tampoco. 3.Él los mira. 4.¿Tú me llamas? Sí, yo te llamo. 5.¿La profesora? Los estudiantes la esperan todos los días. 6.¿Conoce Ud. a Madonna? No, yo no la conozco, pero quiero conocerla (pero la quiero conocer). 7.¿Él va a invitarnos? Sí, él va a invitarlos a todos. 8.¿Compra Ud. muchos regalos? Sí, yo los compro. 9.¿La canción nueva? Angelo puede tocarla en el piano. 10.¿El periódico mexicano? Los estudiantes lo leen en la biblioteca.

21. Indefinite and Negative Words

A. 1.siempre 2.algunos 3.también 4.algunas 5.alguien 6.algo

B. 1.No hay ningún restaurante bueno en nuestra ciudad. 2.Nadie habla ruso. 3.Nunca estudiamos en casa/ No estudiamos en casa nunca. 4.No tienen nada en la mano. 5.Yo tampoco miro la tele los sábados/Yo no miro tampoco la tele los sábados. 6.No quieren ningún sistema para entender los verbos irregulares. 7.No sirven ni tacos ni enchiladas. 8.Nadie prepara la cena ahora. 9.No hay ningún libro en la mesa. 10.Nunca habla francés en su clase de español/No habla nunca francés en su clase de español. 11.Uds. no van a Europa. Nosotros tampoco. 12.¿No le gusta nada?

C. 1.Nosotros no bebemos nada en clase. 2.Yo nunca preparo mi tarea en mi motocicleta/Yo no preparo nunca mi tarea en mi motocicleta. 3.Luis tiene algo en su bolsillo. 4.Nosotros no vamos a Portugal tampoco. 5.Ella no quiere ni café ni té. 6.Alguien lee ahora. 7.Nadie en mi familia habla alemán. 8.Hay algunos hoteles excelentes en nuestra ciudad. 9.¿Hay algunos restaurantes franceses en Santa Bárbara? 10.No hay ninguna clase fácil. 11.Yo necesito alguna manera de terminar este ejercicio rápidamente. 12.Ellos no compran nada.

22. Formal Commands

A & B. Just add an "**n**" to each verb.

C. 1.No coma demasiado. 2.No llegue tarde. 3.Pague sus cuentas. 4.No fume mucho. 5.Beba leche. 6.Repita las explicaciones. 7. No duerma dieciséis horas. 8.No pida sólo ensalada. 9.No salga. 10.No vaya. 11.Traiga. 12.No dé tarea siempre.

D. 1.No pongan 2.Salgan 3.Regresen 4.No cenen 5.Jueguen 6.Digan 7.No almuercen 8.Abracen 9.Saquen 10.Sepan 11.No duerman 12.No lleguen tarde.

E. 1.No la fume. 2.No se quiten. 3.No la escriban. 4.No los abra. 5.No se ponga. 6.No me crea. 7.No los lea. 8.No las practiquen. 9.No las tome. 10.No lo enseñe. 11.No nos busque. 12.No se bañe. 13.No la sirva. 14.No se acueste. 15.No la repita. 16.No me dé. 17.No nos oiga. 18.No se vista. 19.No los hagan. 20.No lo piense. 21.No se levanten. 22.No la empiece. 23.No lo ponga. 24.No le escriba. 25.No lo cierre.

F. 1.Háganlos 2.Sáquela 3.Dígale 4.Sírvala 5.Bébalo 6.Arréglelo 7.Véalo 8.Cómala 9.Llámenos 10.Búsquelo 11.Cántenla 12.Háblele 13.Levántese 14.Báñense 15.Diviértase 16.Acuéstense

G. 1.estudie/n 2.escriba/n 3.empiece/n 4.vuelva/n 5.haga/n 6.póngase/pónganse 7.vaya/n 8.venga/n 9.despiértese/despiértense 10.traiga/n 11.quítese/quítense 12.diga/n 13.vístase/vístanse 14.levántese/levántense 15.pida/n

H. 1.Compre el coche. Cómprelo ahora. 2.Vaya a la escuela. Vaya todos los días. 3.Diviértanse. 4.No salgan esta noche. 5.Vengan aquí el viernes. 6.Levántese. 7.No vendan su casa. No la vendan ahora. 8.No nos busque ahora, búsquenos mañana. 9.No se quite la chaqueta. 10.Empiece sus lecciones. Empiécelas ahora. 11.Alumnos, pongan las plumas en la mesa. No las pongan en su café. 12.Pónganse el suéter. 13.Duerma siete horas, pero no duerma en clase. 14.Venda su motocicleta. Véndala hoy. 15.Pida el bistec y cómalo. 16.Despiértase. 17.No nos traiga sus problemas. 18.Tome dos aspirinas y <u>no</u> me llame en la mañana. 19.No se bañe ahora. 20.Piénselo.

23. Indirect Object Pronouns

A. 1.to the poor students 2.my husband 3.the secretary 4.for the man with the baby carriage 5.students 6.to me 7.us 8.her 9.them 10.you

B. 1.me 2.nos 3.te 4.le 5.les 6.nos 7.te 8.les 9.me 10.nos

C. 1.les 2.le 3.le 4.le 5.les 6.le

D. 1.nos 2.te 3.me 4.les 5.le/le 6.nos 7.me 8.les 9.nos 10.te

E. 1.Sí, yo te escribo. 2.Sí, yo te hablo. 3.Sí, yo te explico la lección. 4.Sí, yo te doy el dinero. 5.Sí, yo te mando tarjetas. 6.Sí, yo te digo la verdad.

F. 1.Sí, yo le mando chocolates. 2.No, yo no le digo mentiras. 3.Sí, yo le presto el dinero. 4.Sí, yo le contesto en español. 5.Sí, yo le sirvo la comida. 6.Sí, yo le explico la lección.

G. 1.No, yo no le digo mentiras. 2.Sí, yo le hablo. 3.Sí, yo les doy dinero. 4.Sí, yo les sirvo el pastel. 5.Sí, yo les canto canciones románticas.

H. 1.Sí, yo les pregunto en inglés. 2.Sí, yo les sirvo las hamburguesas. 3.Sí, nosotros les damos el boleto. 4.Sí, nosotros les compramos regalos. 5.Sí, nosotros les escribimos cartas.

I. 1.Sí, ellos me preguntan. 2.Sí, ella me sirve la sopa. 3. Sí, ellos me dicen la verdad. 4.Sí, él me explica las respuestas. 5.No, él no me trae el café.

J. 1.Sí, ellos te (le) mandan flores. 2.Sí, ellos te (le) hacen el favor. 3.Sí, ellos te (le) compran regalos. 4.Sí, ellos te (le) cantan canciones románticas. 5.Sí, ellos te (le) preparan la cena.

K. 1.Sí, ella nos (les) dice la verdad. 2.Sí, él nos (les) hace el favor. 3.Sí, él nos (les) trae el menú. 4.Sí, ella nos (les) escribe la carta. 5. Sí, ellos nos (les) abren la puerta.

L. 1. Sí, yo voy a darle mi número de teléfono/Sí, yo le voy a dar mi número de teléfono. 2.Sí, yo deseo comprarles regalos/ Sí, yo les deseo comprar regalos. 3.Sí, yo quiero explicarles la lección/Sí, yo les quiero explicar la lección. 4. Sí, nosotros vamos a mandarles chocolates/Sí, nosotros les vamos a mandar chocolates. 5. Sí, yo puedo prestarle el coche/Sí, yo le puedo prestar el coche.

M. 1.doy/les 2.dices/le 3.damos/te 4.dicen/nos 5.dan/les 6.dice/me

N. 1.Sí, yo te escribo en francés. 2.Sí, yo le presto mi coche. 3.Sí, yo les hablo (a ellos) en portugués. 4.Sí, yo les canto canciones italianas. 5.Sí, ellos me sirven la cerveza. 6.Sí, ella te (le) manda flores. 7.Sí, él nos (les) hace favores. 8. Sí, yo quiero darte mi número de teléfono/ Sí, yo te quiero dar mi número de teléfono. 9.Sí, nosotros vamos a comprarles regalos/Sí, nosotros les vamos a comprar regalos. 10. Sí, yo puedo traerle el menú/ Sí, yo le puedo traer el menú. 11.Sí, yo le explico el problema (a él). 12.Sí, nosotros les decimos la verdad (a ellos).

O 1.¿Los estudiantes? Ellos me hablan en inglés, pero yo les contesto siempre en español. 2.¿Donald Trump? Yo le mando un regalo caro. 3.El profesor nos da exámenes fáciles. 4. ¿El doctor? ¿Puede él explicarme el problema?/¿Me puede él explicar el problema? 5.¿La secretaria? Nosotros vamos a decirle la verdad/Nosotros le vamos a decir la verdad. 6.La sicóloga no le va a dar su número de teléfono/La sicóloga no va a darle su número de teléfono. 7.Mi padre nos compra un diccionario muy bueno. 8.¿Los clientes? El camarero les sirve el desayuno. 9.¿Mary? Ella les guarda sus asientos. 10.¿Su primo Jack? Yo nunca le presto dinero. 11.Pedro y yo le podemos hacer el favor a tu tío/ Pedro y yo podemos hacerle el favor a tu tío. 12.¿Va Ud. a prepararles la cena a todos los estudiantes? ¿Les va a preparar Ud. la cena a todos los estudiantes? 13. Mi hermana le abre la ventana a Ud. 14.Los chicos siempre me hacen preguntas difíciles. 15. ¿Don Juan? Carmen no le quiere dar su número de teléfono/Carmen no quiere darle su número de teléfono.

24. Direct Vs. Indirect
Object Pronouns

A. D=Direct; I=Indirect
1. D/money I/to his church 2.I/our son D/a new bike 3.D/an easy exam I/for you 4.I/the doctor D/a big favor 5.D/the door I/for the children 6.D/the difficult grammar points I/to the students 7.D/good classes I/to me 8.D/the competent plumber who speaks Spanish 9.I/to our daughter 10.D/his classmates
B. 1.D/ a sus amigos. 2.D/ cartas 3.D/a los chicos que hablan francés 4.I/nos D/flores 5.I/te D/regalos 6.I/les D/favores. 7.I/te D/mentiritas 8.I/le al doctor D/el problema 9.I/te D/mi coche viejo 10.I/nos D/su motocicleta
C. 1.Ella le hace un favor. 2.Nosotros lo miramos (a Ud.), pero la miramos (a ella) también. 3.Él les compra un regalo muy caro. 4.Los turistas los invitan (a Uds.), pero no la invitan (a ella). 5.Ellos lo esperan. 6.Él la llama. 7.El profesor les abre la ventana (a ellos). 8.Mis abuelos le mandan chocolates. 9.Yo los veo en clase. 10.Ellos le van a escribir una carta larga/Ellos van a escribirle una carta larga. 11.Nosotros queremos pedirle su número de teléfono/ Nosotros le queremos pedir su número de teléfono. 12.Él los ayuda. 13.Su amigo les presta su coche. 14.Yo no la conozco muy bien. 15.Ella no te puede decir todo/ Ella no puede decirte todo. 16.El señor Ortega le da su receta para tamales.
D. 1.¿Mary? Yo no la invito a la fiesta. 2.¿Los chicos? Nosotros no los conocemos muy bien. 3.¿Las enchiladas? Ellos las preparan ahora mismo. 4.¿Las novelas largas? Luis las lee. 5.¿El doctor? Ellos lo llaman pronto. 6.¿El coche nuevo? Frank no lo compra. 7.¿Uds. nos invitan? Sí, nosotros los invitamos. 8.¿Pedro mira a las chicas? Sí, él las mira, pero no las puede ver muy bien/no puede verlas muy bien. 9.¿Ud. busca a su hermano? Sí, yo lo busco. 10.¿El profesor los espera? No, él no nos espera nunca; siempre lo esperamos (a él).

E. 1.Nosotros le cerramos las ventanas. 2.¿El presidente? Nosotros le escribimos una carta larga. 3.¿Los doctores? Yo no les mando dinero. 4.¿El hermano de Pedro? Mary le compra un regalo (a él). 5.¿Los estudiantes? El profesor les hace un favor. 6.¿Los chicos? Las chicas les abren la puerta (a ellos). 7.¿Mis abuelos? Yo les escribo cartas bonitas. 8.¿El papá de Luisa? Ella le sirve enchiladas esta noche. 9.¿Los clientes? El camarero les trae sus ensaladas. 10.¿Los niños? Su maestro les enseña inglés.

F. 1.¿Francisco? Yo le hablo en clase. 2.¿El coche? Necesitamos buscarlo después de la clase/Lo necesitamos buscar después de la clase. 3.¿Los profesores? Linda los invita. 4.¿La casa? Mis padres la venden. 5.¿Los clientes? Los camareros les sirven tamales. 6.¿Las cartas? Los estudiantes las mandan esta tarde. 7.Jennifer y yo le hacemos un favor a su padre. 8.¿Los regalos? La secretaria los trae más tarde. 9.Ellos le (te) abren la puerta. 10.¿Los poemas? Yo no quiero escribirlos/ Yo no los quiero escribir.

25. *Gustar*

A. 1.gusta 2.gusta 3.gustan 4.gusta 5.gusta 6.gustan 7.gustan 8.gustan 9.gustan 10.gustan

B. 1.a/les 2.a/le 3.a/le/gusta 4.a/gusta 5.a/les 6.a/les/gustan 7.a/le/gusta 8.a/les/gusta

C. 1.Me gusta el español, pero no me gustan los exámenes. 2.¿Te gusta bailar? 3.¿A su papá le gusta el vino? 4.No nos gusta cocinar, pero nos gusta comer. 5.¿Le gustan las clases grandes? 6.A Mary le gustan las canciones francesas, pero no le gusta cantar. 7.Nos gustan los coches japoneses. 8.¿A tus hermanos les gustan las películas de horror? 9.Me gustaría ir a Madrid. 10.¿Les gusta la playa? 11.¿A su profesora de matemáticas le gusta la cerveza? 12.¿Al presidente le gustan los reporteros?

26. Preterite

A. 1.hablé 2.estudié 3.miré 4.bailaste 5.terminaste 6.compraste 7.esperó 8.entró 9.pronunció 10.contestó 11.cantamos 12.practicamos 13.miraron 14.entraron 15.terminaron 16.bailamos 17.compró 18.contesté 19.estudiaste 20.entraron

B. 1.hablé 2.miraste 3.cantó 4.bailó 5.terminó 6.esperaron 7.estudiaron 8.pronuncié 9.habló 10.estudió 11.miraron 12.compraron 13.estudiamos 14.cantamos 15.estudiaron 16.miraron

C. 1.escribí 2.abrí 3.recibí 4.comiste 5.saliste 6.abriste 7.bebió 8.asistió 9.vivió 10.comió 11.aprendimos 12.salimos 13.comprendieron 14.comieron 15.vivieron 16.recibimos 17.abrió 18.salí 19.asististe 20.aprendieron

D. 1.comí 2.viviste 3.escribió 4.abrí 5.comiste 6.salió 7.vivió 8.bebió 9.comimos 10.escribimos 11.salimos 12.vivieron 13.bebieron 14.abrieron 15.abrieron 16. conocieron

E. 1.vio 2.busqué 3.volvió 4.dimos 5.fuiste 6.llegué 7.hicieron 8.leyó 9.dio 10.fuimos 11.pensaron 12.creíste 13.empecé 14.fueron 15.vio 16.fuimos

F. 1.llegué 2.fue 3.fueron 4.creíste 5.empecé 6.vimos 7.dieron 8.hizo 9.pensaste 10.volvió 11.fuimos 12.busqué

G. 1.canté/ cantaste/ cantó/ cantamos/ cantaron 2.comí/ comiste/ comió/ comimos/ comieron 3.salí/ saliste/ salió/ salimos/ salieron 4.fui/fuiste/fue/ fuimos/ fueron 5.hice/hiciste/hizo/hicimos/hicieron 6.creí/creíste/creyó/creímos/creyeron 7.pagué/pagaste/pagó/pagamos/pagaron 8.empecé/empezaste/empezó/empezamos/empezaron

H. 1.mandó 2.viví 3.comieron 4.hiciste 5.escribimos 6.empecé 7.pronunciaron 8.dio 9.cené 10.saliste 11.vio 12.fuimos 13.aprendieron 14.recibió 15.estudié 16.fueron 17.terminó 18.asististe 19.creí 20.pagaron

I. 1.Hablo español en casa, pero ayer hablé francés. 2.Bailamos hasta las dos de la mañana. 3.Los estudiantes fueron a clase a tiempo, pero el profesor llegó tarde. 4.Mi padre me llamó de España la semana pasada. 5.La secretaria escribió una carta larga. 6.¿Dónde compraste tu coche? 7.No hice nada la semana pasada. 8.¿Vendieron Uds. sus libros de español el año pasado? 9.Luis salió de casa temprano esta mañana. 10.¿Dónde aprendió Ud. italiano? 11.Vi una buena película anoche. 12.Ella leyó un libro largo. 13.¿A qué hora regresó Ud. a casa ayer? 14.Le dimos un reloj a nuestro padre para su cumpleaños. 15.Él creyó que ella practicó las matemáticas en la fiesta. 16.Pagué cincuenta dólares por mi libro de español.

27. Irregular Preterites

A. 1.vine 2.tuve 3.supe 4.quisiste 5.pusiste 6.estuviste 7.pudo 8.dijo 9.trajo 10.estuvo 11.pudimos 12.pusimos 13.quisieron 14.supieron 15.tuvieron 16.vinimos 17.dijiste 18.traje 19.estuvo 20.pudieron

B. 1.trajo 2.pude 3.pusieron 4.dijiste 5.quisimos

C. 1.Conocí a una persona interesante la semana pasada. 2.Los estudiantes vinieron a clase a tiempo. 3.¿Lo supieron todo Uds.? 4.Mis padres no quisieron comprarme un coche. 5.¿Dónde estuvo Ud. anoche? 6.¿Quién te dijo eso? 7.Puse crema y azúcar en mi café, pero no puse licor. 8.Le trajimos flores a Mercedes al hospital. 9.Ella tuvo un día malo ayer. 10.Yo no dije nada. 11.Él estuvo en la escuela la semana pasada. 12.Nosotros no vinimos aquí ayer. 13.Ella quiso llamarme hace dos horas. 14.Ellos trajeron vino a nuestra fiesta. 15.Hubo un problema con su oche.

28. Stem-Changing Preterites

A. 1.murió 2.me despedí 3.se rió 4.conseguimos 5.se divirtieron 6.siguieron 7.prefirió 8.pediste 9.dormí 10.se divirtió 11.se despidieron 12.sonreímos 13.murieron 14.se vistieron 15.sirvió 16.nos sentimos 17.siguió 18.te dormiste 19.conseguí 20.pidieron

B. 1.se vistió 2.murió 3.se despidieron 4.seguimos 5.se durmieron 6.se rió

C. 1.Nosotros nos dormimos a las nueve de la noche. 2.Mi padre murió hace dos años. 3.Luis se divirtió en la fiesta. 4.María consiguió un nuevo trabajo hace cinco meses. 5.Yo no te pedí dinero. 6.Él se vistió en diez minutos. 7.Ellos se sintieron mal ayer. 8.El camarero nos sirvió buenos tamales. 9.Nosotros reímos mucho en la clase. 10.Ella se despidió y se fue. 11.Ellos sonrieron cuando él les sirvió el café. 12.Mi abuelo murió el año pasado. 13. Nosotros seguimos todas las direcciones. 14.Yo dormí muchas horas.

29. Double Object Pronouns

A. 1.Te las mando 2.Me la canta 3.Te lo prestan 4.Nos lo sirven 5.Te lo pedimos 6.Me las hacen 7.Me la compran 8.Nos las escribe 9.Te la explico 10.Te lo trae

B. 1.Se lo sirvo (a ella) 2.Se la dicen (a él) 3.Se los traemos (a Ud.) 4.Se lo manda (a ellos) 5.Se lo prestan (a ellos) 6.Se lo haces (a él) 7.Se las cantamos (a ellos) 8.Se lo explica (a él) 9.Se los recomiendan (a Uds.) 10.No se las dice (a Ud.)

C. 1.Se la compro (a Ud.) 2.Se la escribo (a Ud.) 3.Se lo presto (a Ud.) 4.Se las mando (a Ud.) 5.Se la sirvo (a Ud.)

D. 1.Te la explico 2.Te las mando 3.Te lo sirvo 4.Te lo pido 5.Te las canto 6.Te la presto

E. 1.No se las digo (a Uds.) 2.Se la sirvo (a Uds.) 3.Se las explico (a Uds.) 4.Se los mando (a Uds.) 5.Se la compro (a Uds.)

F. 1.Se lo explico (a él) 2.Se lo guardo (a él) 3.No se las digo (a él) 4.Se lo presto (a él) 5.Se lo hago (a ella)

G. 1.Se lo doy (a ellos) 2.Se la compro (a ellos) 3.Se los escribo (a ellos) 4.Se la traigo (a ellas) 5. Se lo sirvo (a ellos) 6.Se los mando (a ellos)

H. 1.Quieren escribírmelas/Me las quieren escribir. 2.Deseamos hacértelo/Te lo deseamos hacer. 3.Vas a prestárnoslo/Nos lo vas a prestar. 4.Acabo de mandárselo/Se lo acabo de mandar. 5.Pueden comprártelo/Te lo pueden comprar. 6.No quiero traérsela/No se la quiero traer.

I. 1.Deseo comprársela/Se la deseo comprar. 2.Voy a escribírsela/Se la voy a escribir. 3.Voy a explicártela/Te la voy a explicar. 4.Puedo mandártelas/Te las puedo mandar. 5.Voy a decírselas (a Uds.)/Se las voy a decir (a Uds.). 6.Quiero traérsela/Se la quiero traer. 7.Voy a explicárselo/Se lo voy a explicar.

J. 1.Se lo pido (a Ud.). 2.Se las canto (a Uds.). 3. Queremos dárselo/Se lo queremos dar. 4.Se los traen. 5.Nos la sirve(s). 6.Deseo comprártelos/Te los deseo comprar. 7.Se la explico (a Uds.). 8.Se la dice (a ellos). 9.Te lo presto. 10.Voy a mandárselas/Se las voy a mandar. 11.No se las decimos (a él) 12.Te/Se la abrimos. 13.Se las hacemos/Se las hacen. 14.Puedo escribírtelo/Te lo puedo escribir.

K. 1.¿El dinero? Se lo doy (a él). 2.¿Nuestro nuevo barco? Acabamos de prestárselo?Se lo acabamos de prestar. 3.¿Las cartas largas? Me las escriben. 4.¿El regalo caro? Nos lo manda. 5.¿Nuestro problema? Se lo explicamos (a Ud.). 6.¿El examen final? El profesor puede dártelo mañana/Te lo puede dar mañana. 7.¿Las enchiladas? ¿Se las sirven (a ella)? 8.¿Sus diccionarios franceses? Me los presta. 9.¿El paquete? Ella va a mandárnoslo/Nos lo va a mandar. 10.¿La situación? Voy a describírsela/Se la voy a describir. 11.¿El vino italiano? No te lo traen. 12.¿Las mentiras? No se las dice (a él). 13.¿El Lexus? Se lo compramos (a ellos). 14.¿El dinero para mi viaje a Tahiti? Se lo pido (a ellos). 15.¿Los poemas románticos? No pueden escribírnoslos/No nos los pueden escribir.

30. Imperfect

A. 1.cantaba, cantabas, cantaban 2.miraban, miraba, mirábamos 3.estudiaba, estudiabas, estudiábamos 4.hablaba, hablábamos, hablaban 5.arreglaba, arreglabas, arreglábamos 6.buscábamos, buscaba, buscaban 7.estaba, estabas, estaban 8.tocaba, tocabas, tocaban, tocaba 9.te acostabas, se acostaban, nos acostábamos, se acostaba 10.nos levantábamos, te levantabas, se levantaban

B. 1.vivías, vivíamos, vivía 2.hacía, hacía, hacían 3.leían, leía, leíamos, leías 4.bebíamos, bebía, bebía, bebían 5.insistían, insistía, insistían 6.me dormía, se dormían, nos dormíamos, se dormía 7.te sentías, se sentía, nos sentíamos, se sentían 8.nos vestíamos, te vestías, me vestía, se vestían 9.comprendían, comprendía, comprendíamos, comprendían 10.escribíamos, escribían, escribía

C. 1.estudiaba, estudiabas, estudiábamos, estudiaban 2.tomaba, tomabas, tomábamos, tomaban 3.llegaba, llegabas, llegábamos, llegaban 4.entendía, entendías, entendíamos, entendían 5.recibía, recibías, recibíamos, recibían 6.vendía, vendías, vendíamos, vendían 7.veía, veías, veíamos, veían 8. iba, ibas, íbamos, iban 9.era, eras, éramos, eran

D. 1. Los sábados yo siempre miraba la televisión. 2.Cuando Conchita tenía doce años, ella tocaba el piano. 3.De niño, Luis cenaba temprano. 4.Tú estabas distraído en clase porque pensabas en tu novia. 5.Pedro estaba enfermo. 6.Mucha gente leía mucho. 7.Mientras nosotros íbamos a la escuela, otras personas iban a la oficina. 8.Era la una cuando yo tomé el almuerzo. 9.Ellos pedían la cena cuando nosotros entrábamos en el restaurante. 10.Cuando él estaba en la escuela primaria, él regresaba a casa a las dos de la tarde. 11.Mi padre fumaba. 12.Nuestros abuelos tenían coches grandes. 13.Yo bebía leche. 14.Su hijo se despertaba a la una de la mañana cuando era bebé. 15.Uds. estaban contentos porque toda su familia estaba en casa para Navidad.

E. 1.I 2.I 3.I 4.P 5.I 6.I 7.P 8.I 9.P

F. 1.Pedro tenía doce años cuando llegó a California. 2.Cuando conocimos a la profesora, ya conocíamos a su hija. 3.Tuve que ir al trabajo. 4.Podían comprar el coche nuevo, pero decidieron esperar hasta el año próximo. 5.¿Dónde estuvo la semana entera? 6.Debía estar aquí a las nueve. 7.Al comienzo ella no sabía nada de sus problemas. Luego, cuando los supo, quiso ayudarlo. 8.Quisimos leer la novela entera. 9.Cuando Luis estaba en la escuela elemental, era un buen estudiante. 10.Los niños no quisieron comer las zanahorias.

G. 1.Hacía 2.cantaban 3.estaba 4.tenía 5.esperó 6.apareció 7.vio 8.pensó 9.quería 10.llamó 11.explicó 12.era 13.se sentó 14.charlaron 15.planearon 16.salió

H. 1.eran 2.vivían 3.estudiaban 4.iban 5.pasaban 6.se graduaron 7.fueron 8.asistió 9.conoció 10.se casó 11.fue 12.conoció 13.pasaron

I. Eran las siete cuando por fin salí de casa. Hacía frío, pero había mucha gente que iba al trabajo. A las siete y media llegué a la oficina. Mi jefe estaba enojado. Le dije que no era buena idea enojarse porque es posible enfermarse. Él me contestó que yo era su secretaria y no su sicóloga. Es verdad. La próxima vez que él se enoja, no le voy a dar ningún consejo. Y quizás voy a encontrar otro jefe que me comprende!

31. *Por* and *Para*

A. 1.por 2.por 3.para 4.para 5.para 6.por 7.por 8.por 9.por 10.por 11.para 12.por 13.por 14.para 15.para 16.para 17.para 18.para 19.para 20.por/por 21.por 22.por 23.por 24.por 25.para/por 26.por 27.para 28.por 29.por 30.por

B. 1.Yo perdí mis llaves. Por eso yo entré por la ventana. 2.Ella nunca viaja por barco. Es demasiado caro. 3.¿Cuándo sales para España? 4.Ellos caminaban por la playa cuando yo los vi. 5.Nosotros fuimos al banco por dinero. 6.El doctor va a llegar tarde para mi cita. 7.Los niños no fueron a la escuela por la lluvia. 8.Ella lo hizo por él porque lo quiere. 9.Para el viernes, estudien Uds. el capítulo 8.

10.Ellos corren muy rápidamente para viejos. 11.Nosotros traemos nuestros paraguas por si acaso. 12.Yo siempre tomo un buen desayuno por la mañana. 13.Conchita pagó 200,000 dólares por su casa. 14.Él trabaja para una compañía mexicana. 15. Mercedes estudia para doctora. 16.El libro fue escrito por un escritor famoso. 17.Esos regalos son para ella. Éstos son para Uds. 18.Para el profesor de español *por* y *para* son fáciles. 19.Nosotros estudiamos muchas horas para esa clase. 20.Ellos toman matemáticas por última vez.

32. Familiar Commands

A. Add an "s" to each verb
B. 1.escucha 2.habla 3.mira 4.prepara 5.toca 6.estudia 7.llega 8.termina 9.escribe 10.lee 11.trae 12.duerme
C. 1.no bebas 2.no compres 3.no escribas 4.no mires 5.no cantes 6.no digas 7.no pongas 8.no vengas 9.no hagas 10.no vayas 11.no seas 12.no tengas 13.no veas
D. 1.No la fumes 2.No la escribas 3.No los abras 4.No los leas 5.No las tomes 6.No lo enseñes 7.No nos busques 8.No la sirvas 9.No la repitas 10.No lo pienses 11.No la empieces 12.No lo cierres
E. 1.escríbele 2.sácala 3.repítelas 4.sírvela 5.bébelo 6.arréglala 7.cómpralos 8.cómela 9.llámanos 10.búscalo 11.cántala 12.háblale
F. 1.No te levantes 2.No te bañes 3.No te quites la chaqueta 4.No te laves 5.No te afeites 6.No te despiertes 7.No te diviertas 8.No te vistas 9.No te duermas
G. 1.No me la cantes 2.No me la mandes 3.No me la digas 4.No me la traigas 5.No nos las sirvas 6.No me lo hagas 7.No nos lo prometas 8.No nos lo pidas
H. 1.estudie, estudien, no estudies, estudia 2.escriba, escriban, no escribas, escribe 3.empiece, empiecen, no empieces, empieza 4.vuelva, vuelvan, no vuelvas, vuelve 5.haga, hagan, no hagas, haz 6.ponga, pongan, no pongas, pon 7.vaya, vayan, no vayas, ve 8.venga, vengan, no vengas, ven 9.traiga, traigan, no traigas, trae
I. 1.Compra el coche. Cómpralo ahora. 2.Ve a la escuela. Ve todos los días 3.No salgas esta noche. 4.Ven aquí el viernes. 5.No vendas tu casa. No la vendas ahora. 6.Vende tu motocicleta. Véndela hoy. 7.Sube al avión. 8.Empieza tus lecciones. Empiézalas ahora. 9.Pon la pluma en la mesa. No la pongas en tu café. 10.Duerme siete horas, pero no duermas en clase. 11.No nos busques hoy. Búscanos mañana. 12.Pide el bistec y cómelo. 13.No nos traigas tus problemas. No nos los traigas nunca. 14.Toma dos aspirinas y <u>no</u> me llames en la mañana. 15.Piénsalo. 16.Prepárale la cena a Mary. Prepárasela. 17. Mándanos tu dirección. Mándanosla pronto. 18.Explícales la gramática a los estudiantes, pero no se la expliques en griego.

33. Present Subjunctive

A. 1.cante, cantemos 2.estudien, estudiemos 3.enseñe, enseñes 4.fume, fumen 5.compre, compren, compremos 6.regresemos, regrese, regrese 7.lleves, lleven, lleve 8.mire, miren, miremos 9.baile, bailes, baile 10.llame, llame, llamen
B. 1.comas, comamos 2.vivan, viva 3.escriban, escriba 4.aprenda, aprendan, aprendamos 5.asistamos, asistan, asistamos 6.abra, abramos, abra 7.insistas, insista, insistan 8.venda, vendamos, vendas 9.leamos, lean, lea 10.beban, beba, beban

C. 1.pagues, paguemos, paguen 2.empiecen, empiece, empiecen 3.conozcan, conozca, conozca 4.dé, dé, den 5.sepa, sepas, sepamos 6.ponga, pongamos, pongan 7.digas, digan, diga 8.haya 9.oigamos, oigan, oiga 10.esté, estemos 11.traiga, traigamos, traigan 12.hagamos, haga, haga 13.comience, comencemos, comiences 14.duerma, durmamos 15.puedan, pueda, podamos 16.salga, salgas, salgamos 17.tengan, tenga 18.vengan, vengamos 19.vea, veamos 20.busque, busquen 21.vayas, vayan 22.pierda, perdamos 23.almuercen, almuerce, almorcemos 24.juguemos, jueguen 25.encuentre, encuentren

D. 1.Quieren que yo hable español ahora. 2.Quiero que Ud. me escriba todas las semanas. 3.Los niños quieren que les mandemos regalos. 4.Su primo no quiere que lo llames a las tres de la mañana. 5.Los profesores quieren que los estudiantes estudien mucho. 6.Los doctores no quieren que sus pacientes fumen. 7.Queremos que Uds. vayan a México en avión. 8.Mi mamá quiere que yo pueda tocar la guitarra. 9.No quiero que Uds. beban mucho. 10.El profesor quiere que traigamos los libros a la clase. 11.Su novia no quiere que él salga con otras mujeres. 12. Su esposo no quiere que ella vea a su ex-novio. 13.Quieren que yo sepa nadar. 14.Nuestro doctor quiere que hagamos ejercicio una hora al día. 15.Quiero que conozcas a mi hija.

E. 1.lleguen 2.regresen 3.coma 4.vayan 5.traiga 6.robes 7.se haga 8.sepan 9.explique 10.tome 11.salga 12.aprenda

F. 1.gane 2.pueda 3.dé 4.haya 5.saquemos 6.llegue 7.sea 8.fumen 9.hagan 10.dé 11.esté 12.tenga

G. 1.pueda 2.se levante 3.sea 4.ganen 5.comprendas 6.digan 7.vayan 8.leamos 9.coma 10.quiera

H. 1.venga 2.sepa 3.gusten 4.pueda 5.tengan 6.pueda 7.hable 8.toque 9.sepa 10.esté

I. 1.dé 2.expliquen 3.llueva 4.despierte 5.cierre 6.comamos 7.empiece

J. 1.preste 2.recibamos 3.termine 4.traiga 5.regresemos 6.lleguen 7.pregunte 8.llueva

K. 1.estudie/estudiemos 2.vivan/vivamos 3.lea/leamos 4.quieras/queramos 5.pongan/pongamos 6.vaya/vayamos 7.prefiera/prefiramos 8.jueguen/juguemos 9.sirva/sirvamos 10. sepas/sepamos 11.hagan/hagamos 12.mande/mandemos 13.comience/comencemos 14.salgan/salgamos 15.dé/demos 16.vengas/vengamos

L. 1.No quiero que llegues tarde. 2.El doctor me dice que yo no fume. 3.Es importante que vayamos de vacaciones. 4.Los turistas nos piden que los llevemos al aeropuerto. 5.Les sorprende que yo pueda comer y hablar al mismo tiempo. 6.El presidente no está contento que los periodistas quieran saber todo. 7.¡Qué extraño que haya un elefante en la piscina! 8.Es terrible que el profesor siempre nos dé tarea. 9.Es evidente que Uds. terminaron sus lecciones. 10.No es cierto que los doctores escriban claramente. 11.Es imposible que mi hija lea una novela en treinta minutos. 12. No conocemos a nadie que pueda hablar francés, español y alemán con su perro. 13.¿Busca Ud. al estudiante que sabe tocar la guitarra? 14.La esposa de John trabaja para que él pueda estudiar medicina en la universidad. 15.El secretario viene a la oficina con tal que su jefe haga el café en la mañana. 16.Van al banco en cuanto abra. 17.Va a esperar hasta que yo llegue. 18.Estamos tristes que Conchita esté en el hospital. 19.Me molesta que siempre me pidas dinero. 20.Mi mamá me prohibe que maneje su Maserati.

34. Present Perfect Indicative

A. 1.has,ha,hemos,han 2.he,ha,hemos,has 3.he,has,ha 4.ha,has,hemos,he
5.han,has,ha,han

B. 1.han 2.has 3.he 4.hemos 5.han 6.has 7.ha 8.ha 9.han 10.hemos 11.he
12.has 13.ha/se ha 14.han 15. hemos 16. he 17.han 18.han 19.han 20.ha 21.he
22.han

C. 1.comprado 2.estado 3.visitado 4.cerrado 5.tratado 6.mandado 7.cenado
8.manejado 9.practicado 10.nadado 11.aprendido 12.subido 13.pedido
14.conocido 15.ido 16.hecho 17.visto 18.escrito 19.oído 20.dicho
21.descubierto 22.vuelto 23.muerto 24.resuelto 25.traído

D. 1.he mirado/has mirado 2.ha cantado/hemos cantado 3.ha traído/han traído
4.han abierto/has abierto 5.ha hecho/han hecho 6.hemos visto/ha visto 7.han
servido/has servido 8.he caído/ha caído 9.han dicho/han dicho 10.hemos
puesto/ha puesto

E. 1.¿Has visitado el Japón todavía? 2.¿Han aprendido su lección todavía?
3.Hemos comido en ese restaurante muchas veces. 4.Ya ha comprado un nuevo
coche. 5.El doctor no ha llegado todavía. 6.Hemos estado en México y
Guatemala varias veces, pero nunca hemos estado en Colombia. 7.Ya nos ha
hecho muchos favores. 8.No he descubierto la verdad todavía. 9. Los estudiantes
ya han aprendido muchos verbos. 10.Me han pedido dinero. 11.Le ha dicho la
historia (a él). 12.¿Tu papá ya ha vuelto de Europa? 13.Siempre he sido un(a)
buen(a) estudiante. 14.Mis hijos ya han aprendido a tocar el piano y la guitarra.
15.No hemos abierto nuestros regalos todavía. 16.Es un problema difícil, pero
creo que ya lo hemos resuelto. 17.Se ha caído muchas veces, pero no se ha roto
nada todavía. 18.Los turistas han escrito algunas tarjetas, pero no han escrito
ninguna carta todavía. 19.Este mes ya he comido en restaurantes varias veces.
20.No le hemos hablado todavía, pero queremos hacerlo pronto.

35. Present Perfect Subjunctive

A. 1.hayas, haya, hayamos, hayan 2.haya, haya, hayamos, hayas 3.haya, hayas,
hayan, haya 4.haya, hayas, hayamos, haya 5.hayan, hayas, haya, hayan

B. 1.haya comprado 2.haya estado 3.hayan visitado 4.haya cerrado 5.hayas
tratado 6.haya mandado 7.hayan cenado 8.hayan manejado 9.haya practicado
10.haya nadado 11.hayan aprendido 12. hayamos subido 13.hayan pedido
14.hayas conocido 15.hayan ido 16.haya hecho 17.hayan visto 18.hayamos
escrito 19.hayan oído 20.haya dicho 21.hayas descubierto 22.hayamos vuelto

C. 1.haya cenado/hayamos cenado 2.hayan hablado/haya hablado
3. hayamos comido/hayas comido 4.hayan aprendido/haya aprendido 5.hayas
dicho/hayan dicho 6.haya hecho/hayas hecho 7.hayan escrito/haya escrito
8.hayas vuelto/haya vuelto 9.haya visto/hayamos visto 10.haya conocido/hayas
conocido

D. 1.No creen que yo haya visitado el Japón muchas veces. 2.Es bueno que hayan
aprendido sus lecciones. 3.No es cierto que hayamos comido en ese horrible
restaurante cinco veces. 4.Es posible que ya haya comprado un coche nuevo .
5.No creo que el doctor haya llegado a tiempo 6.Nos alegramos que Ud. haya
estado en México y Guatemala varias veces. 7.Dudan que él me haya hecho
muchos favores. 8.Es imposible que no hayan descubierto la verdad todavía.
9.Niega que los estudiantes ya hayan aprendido muchos verbos.

10.Es lástima que él me haya pedido dinero otra vez. 11.Espero que le hayan dicho la historia. 12.Es probable que su padre haya vuelto de Europa. 13.No es cierto que haya sido mal estudiante. 14.Es increíble que sus hijos hayan aprendido a tocar el piano y la guitarra en tres meses. 15.Dudan que no hayamos abierto nuestros regalos todavía. 16.Espero que hayan resuelto su difícil problema. 17.Es increíble que se haya caído muchas veces y no se haya roto las piernas. 18.Me alegro que los turistas hayan escrito unas tarjetas.

36. Future

A. 1.cantará, cantarás, cantarán 2.mirarán, mirará, miraremos 3.estudiará, estudiarás, estudiaremos 4.hablará, hablaremos, hablará, hablarán 5.arreglaré, arreglarás, arreglaremos 6.buscaremos, buscaré, buscará, buscarán 7.estará, estarás, estarán, estarán 8.tocará, tocarás, tocarán, tocará 9.te acostarás, se acostarán, nos acostaremos, se acostará 10.se levantarán, nos levantaremos, te levantarás, se levantarán 11.viviré, vivirás, viviremos, vivirá 12.leerán, leeré, leeremos 13.beberemos, beberá, beberá, beberán 14.insistirán, insistirá, insistirás, insistirán 15.me dormiré, se dormirán, nos dormiremos, se dormirá

B. 1.te harás, se hará, nos haremos, se harán 2.diremos, dirás, diré, dirán 3.podrán, podrá, podremos, podrán 4.pondremos, pondrán, pondrá, pondrán 5.vendré, vendrás, vendremos 6.tendremos, tendré, tendrá, tendrán 7.saldrá, saldrás, saldrán, saldrán 8.sabrá, sabrás, sabrán 9.querrás/tendrás querrán/tendrán querremos/tendremos 10.se pondrán, nos pondremos, te pondrás

C. 1.estarás, estarán 2. sabré, sabrá 3.cantaremos, cantará 4.hará, harás 5.llegarán, llegaré 6.comerá, comeremos 7.podrá, podrán 8.saldré, saldrán 9.vendremos, vendrás 10.tendrá, tendrán

D. 1.Compraré un coche nuevo el mes próximo. 2.Estarán aquí el año próximo. 3.Vivirá en Colombia en tres años. 4.Arreglará su coche y luego irá a su trabajo. 5.No beberás si manejarás. 6.Tendremos mucho dinero en seis años. 7.Podrán entender el francés en unos semestres. 8.El profesor dará una prueba fácil. 9.No diré mentiritas. 10.Nos levantaremos temprano y entonces iremos de vacaciones. 11.No habrá clases la semana próxima. 12.Saldrá con ella pronto. 13.¿Vendrás a la escuela el semestre próximo? 14.¿Dónde vivirán nuestros padres en cinco años? 15.Escribiré una gran novela.

37. Imperfect Subjunctive

A. 1.hablaras, hablara, habláramos, hablaran 2.comiera, comiera, comiéramos, comieras 3.mirara, miraras, miraran, mirara 4.estudiara, estudiaras, estudiáramos, estudiara 5.cantaran, cantaras, cantara, cantaran 6.leyeran, leyéramos 7.hiciera, hiciéramos 8.fuera, fueran 9.dieran, dieran 10.fueras, fueran 11.estuvieras, estuvieran 12.vinieran, viniéramos 13.quisieras, quisieran 14.pudiéramos, pudieran 15.supieras, supiéramos 16.tuviéramos, tuvieran

B. 1.comprara 2.estuviera 3.visitaran 4.invitara 5.trataras 6.escribiera 7.aprendieran 8.pidieran 9.fueran 10.hiciera 11.oyeran 12.dijera 13.descubrieras 14.durmieras 15.viniera 16.trajera 17.fueras 18.leyéramos 19.estuvieran 20.pudieran 21.tuviera 22.diera 23.dijeran

C. 1.mirara/miraran 2.estudiaran/estudiaras 3.vivieras/viviéramos 4.escribiéramos/escribiera 5.hiciera/hicieran 6.dieran/diera 7.trajeras/trajeran 8.pudieran/pudieras 9.fuera/fuéramos 10.fuera/fueran

D. 1.No creyeron que yo visitara seis países en cuatro días. 2.No era verdad que comiéramos en ese restaurante. 3.Era posible que él comprara un nuevo coche. 4.No creía que el doctor llegara a tiempo. 5.Nos alegramos que Uds. visitaran México y Guatemala. 6.Dudaban que él me hiciera muchos favores. 7.Fue una lástima que ellos me pidieran dinero. 8.Esperábamos que ellos le dijeran la historia. 9.Era probable que su papá regresara de Europa con muchos regalos. 10.Era increíble que sus hijos aprendieran a tocar el piano y la guitarra en tres meses. 11.Esperaba que ellos resolvieran su difícil problema. 12.No era posible que ella se cayera y no se rompiera las piernas. 13.Era importante que él pudiera estar allí. 14.Ellos no creían que hiciéramos toda la tarea en diez minutos. 15.Quería que trajéramos la cerveza a la fiesta. 16.Esperábamos que ellos vinieran a clase a tiempo. 17.Se alegraba que ellos fueran personas amables. 18.Ella dudaba que fuéramos a España sólo por dos días. 19.Los padres temían que los niños quisieran comer pizza otra vez. 20.Era imposible que Ud. supiera todo el vocabulario nuevo. 21.No creíamos que él pusiera sal en el pastel. 22.Esperábamos que el bebé durmiera quince horas. 23.Dudaba que hubiera un examen hoy. 24.Ella sentía que ellos no estuvieran presentes en su boda.

38. Conditional

A. 1.cantaría, cantarías, cantarían 2.mirarían, miraría, miraríamos 3.estudiaría, estudiarías, estudiaríamos 4.hablaríamos, hablaría, hablarían 5.arreglaría, arreglarías, arreglaríamos 6.buscaríamos, buscaría, buscaría 7.estaría, estarías, estarían 8.tocaría, tocarías, tocarían 9.te acostarías, se acostarían, nos acostaríamos 10.nos levantaríamos, te levantarías, se levantarían 11.viviría, viviríamos, viviría 12.lleería, leeríamos, leerías 13.beberíamos, bebería, beberían 14.insistiría, insistirías, insistirían 15.se dormirían, nos dormiríamos, se dormiría

B. 1.te harías, nos haríamos, se harían 2.diríamos, dirían 3. podríamos, podrían 4.nos pondríamos, se pondrían 5.vendrías, vendríamos 6.tendríamos, tendría 7.saldrías, saldrían 8.sabrías, sabría 9.querrían, querríamos

C. 1.estarías, estarían 2.tocaría, tocaríamos 3.insistiría, insistirían 4.nos dormiríamos, se dormiría 5.harían, haría 6.pondría, pondrías 7.saldría, saldrían 8.dirías, diría 9.iría, iríamos 10.tendría, tendrían

D. 1.Hablaríamos español, pero él no entiende la lengua. 2.El estudiante leería toda la novela para mañana, pero es demasiado larga. 3.Vivirían en San Francisco, pero es demasiado caro. 4. Bebería vino, pero me dormiría inmediatamente. 5.Tendría mucho dinero, pero le gusta usar su tarjeta de crédito demasiado. 6.Nos diría todo, pero no lo sabe. 7.Se pondría la chaqueta, pero no hace frío. 8.Te harías rico, pero no te gusta trabajar veinte horas al día. 9.Saldría de casa a las seis, pero no me levanto hasta las ocho. 10.Les darían todo su dinero, pero no sería bastante para pagar todas sus cuentas. 11.Ella vendría a Europa, pero necesita terminar la escuela primero. 12.Nosotros estaríamos en casa ahora, pero tenemos que ver a nuestro profesor de francés. 13.¿Irías a Las Vegas en tren? 14.Yo diría algo, pero tengo miedo de hablar en frente de grupos grandes. 15.Ella me haría un pastel, pero no tiene todos los ingredientes.

39. Review of Verbs

A. 1.miro 2.miraba 3.miré 4.miraré 5.miraría 6.he mirado 7.mire 8.haya mirado 9.mirara 10.mire 11.miren 12.no mires 13.mira

B. 1.lees 2.leías 3.leíste 4.leerás 5.leerías 6.has leído 7.leas 8.hayas leído 9.leyeras 10.lea 11.lean 12.no leas 13.lee

C. 1.dice 2.decía 3.dijo 4.dirá 5.diría 6.ha dicho 7.diga 8.haya dicho 9.dijera 10.diga 11.digan 12.no digas 13.di

D. 1.empezamos 2.empezábamos 3.empezamos 4.empezaremos 5.empezaríamos 6.hemos empezado 7.empecemos 8.hayamos empezado 9.empezáramos 10.empiece 11.empiecen 12.no empieces 13.empieza

E. 1.vuelven 2.volvían 3.volvieron 4.volverán 5.volverían 6.han vuelto 7.vuelvan 8.hayan vuelto 9.volvieran 10.vuelva 11.vuelvan 12.no vuelvas 13.vuelve

F. 1.hablo 2.hablaba 3.hablaba 4.hablé ayer 5.hablaré 6.hablaría 7.he hablado 8.Dudan que yo hable. 9.Dudan que haya hablado. 10.Dudaban que yo hablara. 11.hable 12.hablen 13.no hables 14.habla

G. 1.comes 2.comías 3.comías 4.comiste ayer 5.comerás 6.comerías 7.has comido 8.Dudan que comas 9.Dudan que hayas comido 10.Dudaban que comieras 11.coma 12.coman 13.no comas 14.come

H. 1.escribe 2.escribía 3.escribía 4.escribió ayer 5.escribirá 6.escribiría 7.ha escrito 8.Dudan que escriba 9.Dudan que haya escrito 10.Dudaban que escribiera 11.escriba 12.escriban 13.no escriba 14.escribe

I. 1.sabemos 2.sabíamos 3.sabíamos 4.supimos 5.sabremos 6.sabríamos 7.hemos sabido 8.Dudan que sepamos 9.Dudan que hayamos sabido 10.Dudaban que supiéramos 11.sepa 12.sepan 13.sabe

J. 1.van 2.iban 3.iban 4.fueron ayer 5.irán 6.irían 7.han ido 8.Dudamos que vayan 9.Dudamos que hayan ido 10.Dudábamos que fueran 11.vaya 12.vayan 13.no vayas 14.ve

ABOUT THE AUTHOR

Domenico Maceri (E-mail: dmaceri@aol.com) (Home Page: http://members.aol.com/dmaceri/) was born in Italy where he received his early training in languages. He continued his studies in languages and literatures at Jersey City State College in New Jersey, UCLA, Cal State Northridge, and later completed a PhD in Comparative Literature (Italian, French, and Spanish) at the University of California in Santa Barbara. He is the author of a book on Pirandello as well as a number of articles which appeared in *World Literature Today, Italian Quarterly, Hispania, Teacher Magazine, Mosaic, Italian Journal, The Los Angeles Times, Hispanic Magazine, The Chicago Tribune, Vista Magazine, The Washington Times*, and elsewhere. A regular book reviewer for *World Literature Today*, Dr. Maceri is professor of Romance languages at Allan Hancock College.